IANNIS XENAKIS

THE MAN AND HIS MUSIC

*A conversation with the composer
and a description of his works*

GREENWOOD PRESS, PUBLISHERS
WESTPORT, CONNECTICUT

Library of Congress Cataloging in Publication Data

[Bois, Mario]
    Iannis Xenakis : the man and his music.

    Reprint of the ed. published by Boosey & Hawkes
Music Publishers, London.
    "Bibliography of the writings of Xenakis": p.
    Discography: p.
    1. Xenakis, Iannis, 1922-
[ML410.X45B6 1980]   780'.92'4 [B]   80-12638
ISBN 0-313-22415-3 (lib. bdg.)

Reprinted with the permission of Boosey and Hawkes Inc.

Reprinted in 1980 by Greenwood Press, a division of
Congressional Information Service, Inc.
88 Post Road West, Westport, CT 06881

Printed in the United States of America

10 9 8 7 6 5 4 3 2 1

CONTENTS

BIOGRAPHY

IANNIS XENAKIS was born in 1922, of Greek parents, in Braïla, Rumania, on the Danube, and from the age of twelve he dreamed of devoting his life to music. His early musical studies were mainly with Aristotle Kundurov, pupil of Ippolitov-Ivanov. At that time he was particularly interested in Greek traditional music—that of the Byzantine Church and folk music; and this inspired him to write some choral and instrumental works, which he later destroyed. But already in this modal music he had begun his explorations in timbre and sonority.

Along with his musical studies Xenakis pursued a scientific education that took him to the Polytechnic School at Athens from which he graduated in 1947 with an engineering degree that opened the door to him for a brilliant career as an architect.

In 1947 he left Athens for Paris, where he continued his musical studies under Arthur Honegger and Darius Milhaud. In particular he attended Olivier Messiaen's courses in Analysis and Musical Aesthetics at the Paris Conservatoire, and also learnt from Hermann Scherchen at Gravesano.

At the end of 1947 Xenakis was invited by the French architect, Le Corbusier, to work with him on a number of important building projects, an association that was to last for the next twelve years, and included collaboration with Le Corbusier on his book "Modulor 2". In 1958 Xenakis himself designed the "avant-garde" Philips pavilion at the Universal Exhibition in Brussels.

From 1955 onwards he introduced into music the conception of "clouds" and "galaxies" of events in sound, and calculus and the theory of Probabilities under the name of "Stochastic Music". Later he made use of the mathematical theory of Games which he refers to as "Strategic Music", and finally the theory of Sets and mathematical Logic which he calls "Symbolic Music".

All his musical works are written for normal instruments of the orchestra with the exception of four Compositions of *musique concrète* or electronic music, viz.: "CONCRET PH"—1957, "DIAMORPHOSES"—1957, "ORIENT - OCCIDENT"—1960, "BOHOR"—1962 (on Philips and BAM discs).

In 1965, Xenakis, already settled in Paris, became a French citizen. At the present time (1967) he is Associate Professor of Mathematical and Automated Music at The University of Indiana, U.S.A., and at The Schola Cantorum in Paris.

Xenakis was founder of L'Equipe de Mathématique et Automatique Musicales, known as EMAMu, in the faculty of the Ecole Pratique des Hautes Etudes at the University of Paris. This group consists of mathematicians, electronic engineers, psychologists, philosophers, anthropologists, and professors from the Sorbonne, etc., for the purpose of making a mathematical study of the universal constants in music and for the production of music automatically with the aid of computers and convertors.

XENAKIS

THE MAN AND HIS MUSIC

March 1966. We had just completed together the signing of a contract for the publication of almost the whole of his *œuvre*, and we had decided to put all in order:
the cataloguing, printing, publicity, and the announcement in one of our
information bulletins. This seemed a good opportunity to present, in a fairly exten-
sive form, Xenakis the man himself, his career, likewise his ideas, which are discussed
at great length and sometimes in none too precise terms. For if this man of the avant-
garde has formulated original concepts, these have in fact been introduced to the
public mainly in the form of journalistic newsflashes, radio discussions and in
rather noisy conferences, that is to say in a manner that is superficial and not
conducive to a proper understanding of the varied and complex ideas advanced
by Xenakis himself. Frequently I have witnessed him being plied with questions:
Why this? Explain that! and Xenakis, placed in the dock on a charge of avante-
gardism, answers one question with a few remarks on the fundamental theory of
'groups" and the other on "orphic pythagoreanism", etc. Add to this the man's
naturally quiet disposition which makes his line of thought sometimes difficult to
follow in the case of a listener who is unfamiliar with the spiritual world of Xenakis.
I therefore proposed this meeting. He arrived in the early afternoon, dressed, as
always, informally, his quiet voice, his fine sharp features reminding one a little
of a Modigliani, his normally sad look enlivened from time to time by a prankish
smile that manages to be both malicious and naïve at the same time, all adding up
to the reasonable and generous man that he is.

We spoke for seven hours, a microphone perched nearby, and the following day
edited and cut the material obtained reducing it to the following text, which, if not
well architected (at least up to the eaves!) seems to me now the only way to give a
true and faithful picture of Xenakis.

MARIO BOIS.

THE MEETING OF 4th MARCH, 1966

MB. Tell me the story of your life. You were born in Greece?

X. No, in Rumania, at Braïla, on the Danube, a small town famous for the colonial conquests of its navigators and its Greek merchants. Greece was poor, its people also. My father was a business-man. I have two brothers, one of whom is now a professor of philosophy at Louisiana, the other an architect and painter in Athens. I left Rumania at the age of ten to go to Greece. There I lived on an island at a school run by two masters, one Greek, the other English. The island was called Spetsai, opposite Hydra. Later, in Athens, I studied engineering at the Polytechnic School. During the war I continued my studies and, gaining my degree in 1947, I came to France.

MB. Could one say that the standard of the Polytechnic in Athens is parallel to that of Paris?

X. I don't know, it may have been then.

MB. You did brilliantly in mathematics and science?

X. Yes and no, I was in the anti-Nazi resistance at the time, and was several times in prison.

MB. What about Paris in 1947?

X. I had wanted to live in the U.S.A.; actually I wanted to do two things: music and the study of mathematics and science. Music was something very important to me but not enough for me to live on. I stopped in Paris and there I stayed.

MB. You were married?

X. No, later in '53, still in France. In Paris I took up my musical studies again seriously. After going to several teachers, in 1950 I finally dropped anchor, so to speak, with Messiaen, in his class of musical æsthetics, and there, encouraged by him to continue with him, I found that his analyses opened up wide horizons for me. That was important, that class of Messiaen's! But one can't exist on music and a glass of water. I met Le Corbusier. I helped him with engineering and architectural calculations in Paris. I did this for 12 years up to 1960. In 1950 I had to leave Messiaen. As far as music was concerned I continued on my own in this field for the next 14 years.

MB. Let's talk about Le Corbusier.

X. It was the first time I had ever met a man with such spiritual force, such a constant questioning of things normally taken for granted. I knew a good deal about the ancient architecture and that had been enough for me; he, on the contrary, opened my eyes to a new kind of architecture I had never thought of. This was a most important revelation, because quite suddenly, instead of boring myself with more calculations, I discovered points of common interest with music (which remained, in spite of all, my sole aim). Up to then my architectural and engineering work had been done to gain a crust, but thanks to Le Corbusier I had now found a fresh interest in architecture. One day in 1952 I asked him if I could undertake a complete project with him, and he accepted with enthusiasm. This was the Couvent de la Tourette. I worked on it for three years, making all the plans for it. The solutions to my new problems in architecture which I arrived at were influenced by musical researches I had previously made: for example METASTASEIS, which was a purely musical work, had pointed towards certain approaches in architecture, by means of which in 1956 I was able to design the Philips pavilion for the Brussels exhibition. I did this from ideas dictated by the music of METASTASEIS which had been written in 1953. (For this pavilion Varèse did the music. Le Corbusier arranged the spectacle and I the architecture.)

MB. Why did you leave Le Corbusier?

X. There were disagreements about æsthetic problems, researches, studies and over money; also there were certain psychological questions . . . it was difficult for him to accept my name to the Philips pavilion.

MB. What other buildings did you work on with Le Corbusier?

X. *L'Unité d'Habitation* at Nantes (making use of prefabrication, an idea new at the time), work in India, for example the roofing for the conference hall at Chandigar, and later, plans for an enormous stadium in Baghdad, never realized owing to the revolution in Iraq, etc.

MB. You left Le Corbusier the end of '59. Did your profession as an architect stop there?

X. Not entirely, since for several years afterwards I continued part-time studies for my own satisfaction, and on the other hand I undertook work for a Parisian engineer to earn a living. I did this at home, which was a fortunate state of affairs because it allowed me to carry on with my music at the same time.

MB. Have you now abandoned your involvement with architecture altogether?

X. No. Whenever I have an opportunity to think about the problems of architecture and town planning, I do so. Thus recently I wrote a study on "Urbanism of the Future" with drawings, which was published in Françoise Choay's book "Urbanism, Utopias and Realities". Passages are to be found throughout the pages of all kinds of writers—Owens, Hugo, Marx, Fourrier, Le Corbusier, Engels, Wright, Jules Verne—who concerned themselves with the problems of living in cities.

MB. And your musical studies?

X. As a child at school, and above all at home, with a teacher who came from Russia, a Greek refugee from Georgia, pupil of Ippolitov-Ivanov.

MB. Do you ever conduct your own works? Would you be capable of it?

X. Doubtless, but it doesn't interest me.

MB. Anything further about your musical background?

X. Mine is an odd case: I come from two countries both with an impoverished musical past in the field of 'serious' music. Very meagre in comparison with the musical past of Western European countries. On the other hand folklore and traditional music are much richer than in the West. Granted, the folklore sources borrowed by the Big Five in Russia, by Bartok and Kodaly in Hungary, by Enesco in Rumania were quickly absorbed by the West, but this kind of folklore counts for little with me. In Greece there are traces, vestigial but important, deriving from antiquity. Side by side there is also Byzantine music, that of the Orthodox Church, also very important but quite different from Gregorian, based on untempered systems—no, I'm wrong to say untempered, because Byzantine music is tempered in a different way: it allows for quarter-tones, and temperament exists but in narrower intervals . . . it has existed thus since ancient times. This is a sensibility that is different from that of modern times (i.e. from the end of the Middle Ages up to our own time).

MB. Did you study local folklore and the local musical liturgy?

X. You shouldn't say "local": Byzantine music exists in Yugoslavia, Serbia, Bulgaria, Rumania, etc.

MB. The same?

X. With very close variants. These countries were formerly part of the Greek-Byzantine empire, or under its later influence.

MB. Which was the first or your works to arouse notice?

X. METASTASEIS, in 1955 at Donaueschingen, under Hans Rosbaud. As to the scandal, half of the audience, the young people, were for me, their elders against. Certainly . . .

MB. And in Paris?

X. ACHORIPSIS at the Pleyel in '59 with Hermann Scherchen. Glissandi were not in fashion then as they are now. One lady, sitting near us, said: "among ourselves" (that is to say among the

Serialists) "one just doesn't do that; but after all it's not without interest." Certain critics, such as Clarendon and Pincherle said "anti-music . . . noisy . . . crazy". I had written in the programme mathematical formulae. They took fright. Why be frightened? Mathematical formulae are not monsters; one can tame them much more easily than one thinks, provided that one doesn't in advance create a blockage in the mind.

MB. Who was "for"?

X. I don't know; Messiaen was one: that gave me great moral support.

MB. Among those who supported you from the start there was of course Scherchen . . .

X. Scherchen was a friend, more than that, a father-confessor for me in the solitude I found myself in then. When first in Paris I was isolated on the musical plane. Ranged against me were the "Serialists" and the "Pointillistes", who were opposed to the music of massed sonorities which I had just invented. For several years I was barred from all paths to performances by the avant-garde musical organizations in Germany. Nevertheless, it was there, later, that I began to be known: at Donaueschingen, and later in Munich at a Musica Viva concert, where Scherchen did PITHOPRAKTA early in '57. There it was worse than METASTASEIS, since three-quarters of the audience was "against"; it was a cold public on subscription tickets, who preferred their music served up tepid. All of a sudden in 1960, when Scherchen had just conducted PITHO-PRAKTA, there was, I don't know why, a kind of conversion among the French critics and public. I ought also to mention that in those dark days I met, besides Scherchen and Messiaen, a man who had a certain respect for what I was doing, Pierre Schaeffer. We immediately plunged into theoretical plans: when we were working together with the Research Group of the O.R.T.F. he accused me of being a Pythagorean and I charged him with being an artisan. You can well see how things are among people who are passionate about their ideas. But I shall never forget those years.

MB. And the Domaine Musical?

X. Goléa mentioned in one of his books that the Domaine Musical had never performed a single work of mine in 10 years. As a result they performed HERMA in '63 and then EONTA towards the end of '64.

MB. Which important conductors have done your works, and which do you consider were the most telling performances as far as you are concerned?

X. First of all, Rosbaud, when he gave METASTASEIS in 1955 at Donaueschingen; then Scherchen with PITHOPRAKTA in March '57. Then, little by little they all began to perform me: Foss, Schuller, Maderna, de Carvalho, Bernstein, Rovicki, Bour, Hadzidakis, Copland, Markowski, Simonovic, Le Roux, Boulez, Maceda, Amy, Bruck, Ozawa, Masson, etc.

MB. Has a ballet ever been made to one of your works?

X. I wrote the music for the tragedy "The Suppliants" which was by definition partly choreographic, for the Greek Theatre at Epidaurus; and then the music for the "Oresteia" in the U.S.A. this year.

MB. Nothing for ballet proper?

X. Béjart has mentioned that he would like to do something.

MB. You and I met Balanchine together.

X. I admire him greatly. I have seen some of the things he did in 1927, which have a remarkable precision and geometrical form. He did say to Nabokoff that he would like to do something of mine. At the moment he is ill. We shall have to see.*

MB. Does Stravinsky know your work?

X. Yes, for some time. I met him a long time ago at the home of a lady who lived in the 16th arron-dissement. It was Pierre Souvtchinsky who introduced me. I saw him again in Berlin when he directed Elegy to J.F.K. He complimented me on my music. Robert Craft wrote recently that I was the most interesting of the "coming composers".

*It is confirmed that Balanchine is currently choreographing Metastaseis and Pithoprakta

MB. You have been a French citizen since May 1965?

X. Yes.

MB. You previously understood that you became a Frenchman in September 1965. You were one for 6 months without knowing it! What made you settle in Paris rather than London or New York?

X. Paris is a kind of contemporary Athens. France is without doubt the country closest to my way of thinking and behaviour. And then there is a strong historic link with Greece.

MB. A link for which you have a feeling?

X. Certainly. The past counts for much with me—links with the past. I have no sympathy with those who reject it. For me it's a question of sensibility.

MB. Do you think that there are other towns more creative in the musical field than Paris?

X. I don't know, but it is difficult to imagine where I could work other than in Paris. Nevertheless for me material conditions for existing have been entirely non-existent in Paris. It has not been on French, but, above all, on American money that I have been living these past four years in the form of commisions and grants, Ford Foundation, for example. The Berlin Senate offered me a house, a tiny Marienbad—most luxurious; though Berlin itself is dead enough from the point of view of musical activity.

MB. What prizes or commissions have you had?

X. AKRATA for the Koussevitsky Foundation, and 3 works commissioned by R.T.F. At present I am engaged on the music for Aeschylus' "Oresteia" for Ypsilanti, a small town in the United States where they present ancient drama in a Greek Theatre (neo-Greek!) I even gained a prize set up in Athens by Hadzidakis, a Greek composer of light and film music. I would think this an example unique in the annals of music of a rich composer dipping into his own pocket to help his brethren in the field of 'serious' music.

MB. Have you any pupils?

X. Young people often come to me. I refuse. I have no pupils except, on occasion, a composer-pianist, Takahashi, whom I met in Japan. Now he plays EONTA, is 27 years old, a composer remarkable in his tastes, his thought and his musical perspective. I am quite sure he will do great things.

MB. Is there a contemporary Japanese school of any merit?

X. When I went there in 1961 the Japanese school was still under the influence of serialism. There were, besides, two principal figures: Matsudaira, père, who composed traditional folk-style music tinged with Western accents, and Mayuzumi, whom I had known in Paris, a pupil of Tony Aubin. Among the younger men the tendency was towards serialism; then after this period a few followed Cage, who had paid a visit the following year, a few followed me and yet others followed both. I also knew Matsuchita, professor of mathematics at Osaka, who is also a composer. Toru Takemitsu and T. Ichiyanagi are original talents of genuine Japanese music.

MB. How does the musical avant-garde in the United States appear to you?

X. I have met with a vitality that seems to me to augur well for the future among certain musical circles. For example at Tanglewood. At this time it was directed by Copland: the nicest possible atmosphere, imbued with a deeply sympathetic kind of humanism. I knew Gunther Schuller there, who introduced me to the U.S.A.; he has his eyes and ears open to everything that is going on. Lukas Foss also. Then Earl Brown and Jerry Hiller; and of course Cage, whose music I know and whom I met at the performance of one of his ballets at the Lincoln Center. I respect him as a person. By way of compensation I saw the Happenings, part of the old New York tradition of some 15 to 20 years' standing.

MB. Let us move on now to another part of our discourse. Let us speak of the technical difficulties of your works. Why are they so hard to play?

X. Because the simple game, the easy style belong to an aesthetic and to a conception of music that are no longer real.

MB. Why?

X. Because our mode of perception, our mode of thought have changed, and consequently so has our mode of action. One can come to love Bach, to appreciate Debussy, Beethoven and other masterpieces from the past, but one cannot do as they did because what we do can no longer follow the same design, the same criteria, the same patterns. As regards the listener, there are two categories: the one that listens with pleasure to contemporary music, and who will listen to and select certain works from the past, in this case it is an actual (real) point of view which is projected into the past. With the listener of the second category, his education belongs to the past. If he embarks on the contemporary he will have a bar to cross: either he will pass or he won't. There are those who remain entirely in the past, through lack of discrimination of present-day music. They are not interested in it because they are ignorant of it or because their education has removed them too far from it. I am not speaking merely of education in the family circle or in school, but of the education of the masses by those enormous distributors of propaganda and information, television and radio, at the disposition of the state or private organizations, whose activities are reactionary and baleful: deforming the ear and the taste, and deforming to monstrous proportions. What would you? The Christians had already understood this, the Communists followed suit, and likewise the Nazis: that if you hammer a nail into someone's head for long enough it won't come out: if one's antennae are focussed from morning to night on the "box" there's no room for anything else. Radio and TV commercials are dictated by money. Though in its specialized transmissions some exception can be made for O.R.T.F.

MB. How do you account for the fact that a sincere amateur, who is not lazy can allow to co-exist in his taste the pleasure of the simple music of a Mozart and the complex music of a Xenakis?

X. An action may be very simple, but very difficult if one has never done it before: one must foresee the period of learning. Actions which appear simple, the classics, are in reality most complex (in the sphere of dancing, Claire Motte will appreciate that, I think). One should speak rather of the transposition of the difficulty, of a new difficulty of simple things.

MB. Would you be capable of writing a piece of music that is simple yet interesting?

X. Simple? What does that mean?

MB. In this context I mean easy to play.

X. That's all I ever do! I remember having presented the score of METASTASEIS in 1956 to a director of the radio: It's impossible" he said, "it needs 40 rehearsals". A short time previously Rosbaud did it on 4 rehearsals, and later Maurice le Roux on 2. So you see, the orchestra learns the actions, which are basically easy. One only has to set to work with a different outlook.

MB. When you write do you indulge in wilful aggressiveness?

X. Decidedly no. Each time I am surprised by the public which reacts badly, violently, believing itself assaulted, violated, duped, or dumbfounded by an astonishing persecution complex.

MB. Nonetheless, when Stravinsky, in his ardent youth, sat down in 1911 to write the first sketches of SACRE don't you really think that he wanted to send the clutter of the past packing and to shake people up?

X. I know that Varèse used to say: "All right, you've got to shake them up, muck 'em about a bit, put a firework under them"—a typical remark of his. No, what I'm aiming at is not so much to tread the beaten track as to feel things, think them and then express them; that's all. That's not the same thing as to be aggressive at all costs. Naturally anything that is new, in sound or any other medium "aggresses". But in these days one has to do a lot to shock, because people expect anything and believe anything possible.

MB. A critic recently wrote about you: "it is a species of desensitized music, but perhaps therein lies the future of the art". Do you compose without sentiment?

X.   Yes, if by sentiment you mean that kind of traditional sentimental effusion of sadness, gaiety or joy. I don't think that this is really admissable. (In my music there is all the agony of my youth, of the Resistance and the aesthetic problems they posed with the huge street-demonstrations, or even more the occasional mysterious, deathly sounds of those cold nights of December '44 in Athens. From this was born my conception of the massing of sound events, and therefore of stochastic music.) Given the standpoint where we are at present in 1966, that would make no sense. In the 19th Century there was a recognized and codified language: a springy rhythm 'signified' gaiety, a rhythm of chordal progressions with chorus—that was a funeral hymn for Victor Hugo, etc. There were social conventions which have vanished and have not been replaced. In consequence sensibility has no longer any conventions by which to express itself. It expresses itself by other means, and it is sensible since it does so express itself; besides, traditional means of expression change very quickly, just as fashion does. Look at pre-war films: how far removed from them are the film techniques of today. In the realm of sensibility our age, the age of speed, is more temperate; I do not think that this sensibility is necessarily the poorer or the less profound, since it seems to me to speak more sincerely with a more truthful tongue. What appears to me to be more important as regards music itself, at any rate in mine, is its abstract nature, its combinatory aspect, in the sense of the ratio of its proportions. Debussy wrote about Rameau, whom he admired: "Perhaps he made a mistake in writing about his theories before composing his operas, for his contemporaries thereby found the opportunity to deduce a complete absence of emotion in his music".

MB. You say your music is abstract. Do you consider that in the 20th Century, so far as concerns aesthetics, music follows 20 years behind painting? If you create an abstract are you not reliving a period corresponding to the years 1910-1920 in painting?

X.   Quite the opposite: music is actually in advance of and has overtaken painting. After the miscarriage of abstract painting—after putting the lid on the Abstract, painting came to a kind of romanticism, with the worship of action; a confidence, a faith in action which they termed "freedom by action". Freedom from what? One doesn't know, but in the final analysis, one calls it "chance", the "aleatoric", "tachism", it doesn't matter what. This terminology is a fashionable error which will pass. What does not pass, and has not passed since pre-history is the constant rational questing in the arts; that is imperishable, it lies dormant or it dominates according to the epoch, but it is always there. In brief, today certain musicians are attacking the problems in a new and positive manner which is preparing the ground for very important tomorrows, but I don't see what painters are preparing for.

MB. How does a work come to you?

X.   I have to live with the thing I am making. I prime it by an aural image, or even by an optical one; ideas come, then take over, or on the other hand retreat. Basically, I don't know at all how that happens; sometimes a result is written unexpectedly, I examine it and say to myself: "I had thought it was going to be something else". Frequently I first of all make some calculations in order to fix the ideas; it doesn't stay like that but I feel that the work has begun. Or again, I make sketches and at the same time drawings.

MB. And the orchestrations? EONTA for example?

X.   Boulez asked me to do something. I said to him "I will do a piece for piano and brass". In that case it was the sonority that interested me before writing a single note.

MB. When do you use the IBM machine?

X.   I haven't used it for all my compositions: only for one family: ATREES, ST 10, ST 48, The String Quartet ST 4, part of STRATEGIE and part of EONTA. There is one family of works.

MB. Why do you use a machine for calculating?

X.   In '56-'57 I wrote ACHOHRIPSIS for orchestra: this work is a sort of reply to a fundamental question, relating as much to aesthetics as to philosophy, that I had been asking myself for a long time: can one construct, is there a way of constructing a work controlled on a general plan by a minimum of rules of composition? I gave the answer at that time after a long period and much research, in a theoretical way, by the calculus of probabilities which I then used for a work which I called ACHOHRIPSIS. Quite suddenly it became apparent to me that, since this thing had been entirely resolved by calculus it would be possible to work a machine which would make the calculations instead of me. What is interesting about the machine? First of all, to objectify this thesis. Next to explore with great ease those parts which would be difficult or impossible as regards the time taken to make the calculations; equally it is to test whether a philosophic thought could have its counterpart in sound and be, or become, an object interesting from the point of view of sound. Finally, the interest is in creating a form of composition which is no longer an object in itself, but an idea in itself, that is to say a possible family of works. There then, thanks to a complex of formulae and logical steps of reasoning, are the data and the necessities that have obliged me to use the computer IBM 7090.

MB. I have heard one of your colleagues explain your process of composition. According to him you feed into the machine the elements (what you call a programme); the machine gives you the possibilities of combinations, and you then choose from among them in order finally to write your work.

X. It isn't that at all; that would be nonsense. No. One must be able (the interest lying in achieving an aim by tethering one's mind to the exactions of the problem) to produce an edifice, to produce an abstract structure by formulae and logic which, dressed as music in the garb of sounds, must be interesting to the very end. This is the bet: that this "thing" must first of all be an original thing, that is to say without precedent, and that it must be interesting. A new thing is always interesting just because it is new, but it can be either deeply or superficially original. I furnish the machine with a very precise tissue of instructions, tightly bound with formulae and reasonings —a whole chain of them—it is this in effect which constitutes the "programme". Then one fixes the input data, which provides you with a kind of "black box". It does its work and gives you certain results. You alter the input data and switch on again: the results are different. The latitude of these input data can be very great or very weak, that depends on you. There is then an arbitrary choice of your point of departure, but the structure doesn't change—the abstract structure. So, from that point of view there is a mixture of the *a priori* and of what is arbitrarily chosen: the former corresponding to the programme and the latter to the input data. This business of machinery, of stochastic, probabilist clockwork which I do, for example for this particular family of works, is really a species of mental imaginary clockwork which may result in works for solo instrument, for choir, perhaps for a complete orchestra, or as I did with STRATEGIE, for two orchestras. You have great freedom of choice. You may use no matter what instrument in a limited range, or on the contrary in the full richness of all its potentialities. You may also affect the structure of the work by giving it, for example, a greater or lesser density (lots of notes, or very few) in deciding the apportioning of these notes, their shades and colours in such and such an area of sensibility, and finally in the total scheme, in the form. There are all kinds of possibilities, but one must get inside the clockwork to understand what all the potentialities of the data are. This language of the machine is universal but I admit that it demands a knowledge that musicians do not ordinarily possess.

MB. What comes out of the "black box"?

X. I arrange meticulously by hand the material received, following exactly the same theoretical principal which holds sway inside the black box; that is to say a living box, which is in some degree fixed at the output of the principal box. I have approximately 10% of decisions still available to me at the output, except for ATREES, in which, wishing to marry together two modes of composition I allowed myself a larger degree of intervention at the output.

MB. There are no works which you leave "raw" as they come out of the machine?

X. No, because one must at least decode the results and transcribe them into traditional notation for the orchestra. Furthermore, the machine often gives solutions that are unplayable on the practical level.

MB. If you had at your disposal an imaginary ideal machine, would you take whatever it gave you in its natural state?

X. If the final result were interesting, I would keep the lot, but one must insist on an interesting result, that is to say a kind of mental kaleidoscope, stochastic if you like, which should be of worth throughout and at every point; then, to have such an object is marvellous from the abstract point of view, a theoretical study entirely abstract, comparable to the power of fashioning an entirely original living being, alive and living under all circumstances of life.

MB. Can you define the term stochastic?

X. It was first used by the Swiss, Jacques Bernoulli, one of the inventors of the Calculus of Probabilities. At the beginning of the 18th Century he wrote a book in Latin called Ars Conjectandi in which he promulgated for the first time the fundamental law of large numbers: he used the term "stochastic" since the law of large numbers implies that the more numerous the phenomena, the more they tend towards a determinate end: the first rule of determinism, the first time that a strait-jacket had been placed around the problems of chance; it's really very important. The word stochastic comes from the Greek, meaning point of aim, target. It's worth noting that in modern as well as ancient Greek this same word also means "to reflect, to think", which is understood thus: to concentrate one's thought on a point of aim, to select something as a target. It was I that introduced the word into musical composition.

MB. Have you written any aleatoric music?

X. No: "aleatoric", in fact "musical improvisation", means that one leaves the choice to the performer. For myself this attitude is an abuse of language and is an abrogation of a composer's function. Complete freedom of choice, as in the case of Cage, says in effect "do what you like, at any moment, no matter how". More restricted freedom, as with Boulez, offers several possibilities of playing several strands and asks the player to choose.

MB. But your work STRATEGIE?

X. STRATEGIE is another matter, it's a "game". The two conductors of the two orchestras which are playing the match have six basic cards to play from which they must choose; in all there are 19 possibilities for each one. But the music that is played thus is not improvised, it is conditioned by the rules of the game, by the established matrix of the game; that is to say the control exercised by the composer goes as far as the choice, which may seem to be improvised; but it never is, because if the conductor of one orchestra chooses a bad card, he pays for it in the later development of the game at the price fixed by the composer. In following the rules of the game the contestants show the conditioning which the composer exercises on their choice, and this is fundamental because in this way that choice does exist. It is a constant dialogue between three people, the two conductors and the composer. There is no abrogation of the composer's function, as with "aleatoric" music where you get either partial or total abrogation, which is absurd.

MB. You have written another work of this genre: DUEL.

X. Based on this same principle. The duel between two parties causes one to be the winner and one to be the loser. These two works are games: in the mathematical theory of "Games" there is the term "duel"; it is a particular case of a large family of games, which, from the mathematical point of view, is not completely resolved.

MB. Is there any aesthetic or philosophical interest in these games?

X. Certainly. It is an extension of the problem of choice; a man's choice depends entirely on himself, on his capacities, faculties, etc. The least of his actions is a choice, the moment he acts he has chosen, it is over. One chooses without stopping. Moreover, it is interesting to create a conflicting situation which is put into relief by a reality, the ruling of the game. The field of experience in this domain is enormous and fascinating. Unfortunately, I have just begun, and far greater means are needed really to explore this wholly uncharted country. It is important from the standpoint of a psychological musical act, and more generally an aesthetic one. Everything is a kind of game, there are philosophies which hold that all life is a game, from the child to the ruler.

MB. It's true that the young Pascal's calculating machine was first of all a toy to him. Montherlant considers that life should be lived as a game, and cites Schiller's phrase "Man is the full man only when he is playing".

X. Doing mathematics, physics, it's all a game; doing something we are passionate about is a game, doing something that doesn't interest us is a game in reverse, one is forced into it, otherwise one loses something else.

MB. One "plays" music . . .

X. "One plays" mathematics, "one plays" atomic bombs: one person makes it, another receives it, the whole of society and its game blends with creation. The god of the Jews played at creating the world in seven days. Plato in the Timaeus says that the Creator fashioned the world in his own image, beginning with Chaos, first the ideal world and following the ideal, the real world. What is the necessity for this creation? It is born of the fact that he created in his own image, because his own image was harmonious.

MB. In relation to PITHOPRAKTA and METASTASEIS the term *musical architecture* has been used, of the construction of musical buildings; when you compose do you search for forms which correspond aurally to planes, curved surfaces, or to be still more precise, to pediments, to roofs, to columns . . .? Your long glissandi have often been taken by listeners as representing slanting planes.

X. Yes, in the particular case of METASTASEIS which corresponds fairly exactly with the architecture of the Philips Pavilion at Brussels, architecture whose surfaces were brought about by moving straight lines (called ruled surfaces). But in a more general sense one can't maintain that architecture is petrified music, or conversely that music is architecture in movement. I have been accused of thinking not as a musician but rather as an architect; it's possible; but one should think of music as an organization in time, and then look for an equivalent organization in space. Take as an example a classical facade, a porch (a rectangle in height, an entrance with bell-tower in a spire or a dome, or a roof, etc.). Notice that with these data you can vary the disposition and proportions ad infinitum. Music may be looked at from this angle. Most frequently musicians start with a detail, of the theme for example, and bring into play the processes of development, of polyphony, of harmony and construct an entire work from very small beginnings: first theme, second theme, counter-subject, modulation of one, kind or another this or that counterpoint, change of orchestration etc. But as soon as you broach entirely new structures and begin to work on them, you can't even try to begin with this or that, and then develop it, because such a process would lead you nowhere. You must on the contrary find a way of looking at, of feeling things of reasoning that is entirely new, and the first thing to do is to establish an overall view of the work, and afterwards to choose your material working at its elements one against another, conjointly or independently, until it becomes organized, vital. In this way this work resembles that of an architect, or more correctly of a sculptor.

MB. So you can't say that, during the course of your composition, at each moment you are searching for a certain musical form that will exactly represent a certain form in space?

X. Never. It is entirely on the abstract plane that that happens; a musical thing must be a living organism, it must have a head and arms; it would be better to speak of biology than of architecture. In music space is not three dimensional, it is multi-dimensional.

MB. You must be aware that your mathematical procedures of composition are absolutely incomprehensible for the listener. I dare say 99% of listeners, and even of musicologists who have done their home-work, or of the technically best equipped composers, understanding nothing of your calculations—Messiaen, Goléa, Rostand have often affirmed this. Do you allow that one can listen to you without involving oneself with your mathematics?

X. The most beautiful girl can only give what she has . . . But I'm sorry about it, these are questions that I ask myself and those who listen, and I wish I could find an answer, not on just that aspect of what I propose, but on the whole thing, that is to say on the thought itself which is contained in each work on the thesis which I pose: I am pretentious on that score: each one of my works poses a logical or philosophical thesis.

MB. What reply do you look for?

X. There you have pinpointed, and I congratulate you on it, a subject which has never been penetrated, that of the very essence of music; what is its role, its aim in present-day society? One might say "it's to pass the time", or "it's for pleasure", or "it's a spiritual diversion" when evaluating the nobility of classical works. For contemporary ones "free intellectualism, exploration of the unknown, etc." The Pop song brings large rewards because it is consumed by the masses, it enters their souls, their lives and stops there; one can very well do without the musical questings of the avant-garde, one already has the musical past of Europe, which is not so bad; people keep discovering old bits of nonsense, mummies that they've dug up, and to hear all that could last a life-time, so what's the point of taking the prickly risks of a sortie into the contemporary world? Musical exploration today is in the same state that mathematics was 80 years ago, when they were considered a crazy fantasy. When Riemann started non-Euclidian geometry, people said it was a freak. Now the result of these scientific researches is tangible enough today, and spectacular in the cosmic field.

MB. What consequences could musical research such as yours have in the distant future?

X. There are two answers to that. First of all, if one approaches music in the same way that I approach mine, it marches with and intermingles with mathematics. Mathematicians are beginning to appreciate this interaction and to react to it, making new propositions most beneficial on the purely material plane. It is the widening of the horizons of the pioneers which gives birth to applications that are profitable to all. The second answer concerns the importance that music can play in the achievement of man through his creative faculties. If one allows these faculties the opportunity to develop, the whole of society is affected, and this will give to humanity an even richer knowledge, and therefore an ever greater mastery.

MB. Teilhard de Chardin expressed the hope that "the age would come when man will be more preoccupied with knowing than having".

X. Music is certainly a basic tool for helping to fulfil this hope. Pythagorism was born of music. Pythagoras built arithmetic, the cult of numbers, on musical foundations. This is splendid; it is Orphic. In Orphism music fulfils the function of the redeemer of souls in their escape from the infernal cycle of reincarnations. If one wishes to be reborn on a higher plane one must look after one's soul. This is to be found also in Homer; it is the Orphic thesis. It is for religious reasons therefore that Pythagoras discovers the processes whereby music is made, and then the relation between length of string and note, and following that the association between sounds and numbers; moreover, as geometry was being born at that same period, Pythagoras interested himself in it. By adding arithmetic to it he laid the foundations of modern mathematics; thus he was able to invade the realm of astronomy, invent the theory of the spheres, the theory of the music of the spheres, of the harmony of the spheres, which survived right up to Kepler; the Keplerian discoveries could never have been made but for the contribution of Pythagoras. In the old days music therefore became, quite simply, a branch of mathematics. Euclid wrote an entire book, called "Harmonics", in which he treated music on the theoretical level. This was the position in the West right up to the Middle Ages: up to the end of the 9th Century, when Hucbald, in his Musica Enchiriadis was analysing plainchant and speaking of music in ancient classical terminology. With the appearance of polyphony, there occured a divorce. Today there are fewer reasons for upholding this divorce than for suppressing it.

MB. Isn't this to go against the stream in a reactionary way, which would be rather odd for a composer of the avant-garde, to hold that the mathematical theories of Pythagoras were engendered from a music that preceded them, and then today, 25 centuries later, to maintain that music should go back to mathematics?

X. Not at all. Music is by definition an art of montage, a combinatory art, a "harmonic" art, and there is plenty to discover and to formulate in this domain. I think I have defined two basic structures, one which belongs to a temporal category in musical thought, the other is independent of time, and its power of abstraction is enormous: ancient music was based on the extra-temporal, which allowed it to be conjoined to mathematics; present-day music, since it is polyphonic, has almost entirely dispensed with the extra-temporal factor in music, to the advantage of the temporal . . . the combination of voices, of modulations, melody, all this is made in time. This music has lost, for example, all that it possessed of modal structure, which was based on tetrachords and "systems" and not on the octave scale; it has lost all that to the advantage of the temporal, that is to say of time-structures.

It is urgent now to forge new ways of thinking, so that the ancient structures (Greek and Byzantine) as well as the actual ones of the music of western countries, and also the musical traditions of other continents, such as Asia and Africa, should be included into an overall theoretic vision essentially based on extra-temporal structures.

MB. Since music gave birth to mathematics, ought it now to seek refuge in a return to mathematics?

X. It isn't a refuge that music asks of mathematics, it is an absorption that it can make of certain parts of mathematics. Music has to dominate mathematics, and without that it becomes either mathematics or nothing at all. One should remain in the realm of music, but music needs mathematics for they are a part of its body. When Bach wrote the Art of the Fugue, he produced a combinatory technique which is mathematical. In this new kind of music which I am propounding, and which at present is no more than the first hesitant stammering, mathematical logic and the machine will give a formidable power in the context of an extremely wide generalization. Did you know that at the age of 16, in 1938, I tried to express Bach in geometrical formulae? . . . but the war came . . .

MB. I want to come back to the public which is listening to you in the concert-hall: there they all are, creasing up their foreheads over your programme-note where, in presenting your work you cite Poisson's Law which you follow up with several algebraic equations. Why do you bother to do all this? Aren't you being a bit of a tease?

X. If the listener doesn't understand any of it, it is first of all useful to show him to himself as ignorant. Because the laws which I cite are universal ones and treasures of humanity, real treasures of human thought. To be unwilling to know them is as uncivilised as to refuse to recognise Michelangelo or Baudelaire. Furthermore, these formulae, which 10 years ago were the property only of the specialist, are now the common property of the average student of elementary mathematics. In a few year's time they will be in every schoolboy's satchel. The level of learning, this also evolves. There exists an inner beauty in mathematics, beyond the enormous enrichment that it brings to those who possess it, even a part of it; pure mathematics approaches poetry.

MB. When I was doing higher mathematics, I was fascinated by imaginary numbers, because they seemed to me to belong to the province of pure poetry. The ephemeral journeys which are made into the country of those numbers whose square is a negative quantity, seemed to me unreal. Are not the deepest mathematical realities outside humanity?

X. No, there is no reality outside humanity. There is no absolute in mathematics: mathematics are a hypothesis, an arbitrary conception that rests on certain axioms that man has chosen from among others, on which he has based the mental machinery of his logic. You see, it's a matter of entirely human construction. A certain logic, that propounded by Aristotle, is extended, becoming today universal, of value to all and applied by them to the experimental or phsyical field. Such a hypothesis, such a physical theory serves its purpose, then a couple of generations later it is refuted, abandoned and replaced by another, which may be complementary or even sometimes contradictory, and this is evolving all the time.

MB. What does mathematical logic provide you with in the matter of your musical composition?

X. It is a working tool, a universal language, an achievement, happiness, a joy in the abstract game.

Obviously there is something else in music, be it a sheen or an embellishment that mathematics does not have. Don't ask me to define music solely in mathematical terms. These two "arts" cannot be identified with each other, cannot be placed one above the other, only they fuse, having certain aspects in common, but there is neither implication nor equality.

MB. The golden number, in architecture, is a human invention?

X. Certainly.

MB. But haven't men in past times believed in the magical value of numbers?

X. Naturally, in the history of human ideas, progressions such as the golden number, magic squares, geometrical figures and all kinds of mathematical and astrogical totems have played a very important part in the arsenal of sorcery. I don't believe in them.

MB. Except in transposing the idea, like Paul Klee, and adding into the vertical and horizontal columns of his magic squares, not figures whose sum is constant, but colours! In the musical milieu your mathematical ideas are generally accepted with closed eyes. Thus, regarding your book "Musiques Formelles" one of my friends, a graduate in mathematics, told me this volume of 300 pages could have been written in 10.

X. There are in my book some mathematical propositions which are very simple, quite elementary, but I had to make myself clear to uninformed readers, and finally to musicians. I didn't abbreviate it because it is not a book on mathematics, but one which makes use of mathematics in applying them to the field of music. The calculations I use are not wrong, that's all; but in fact I don't think that the mathematics I make use of have much relevance for mathematicians, who in general do not know much about music. However, the method employed and the problems raised could help them to get away from their often desiccating specialization. There should be collaboration with these people, and one mustn't forget that people who understand mathematics cannot necessarily understand its relationship with music. It was in this context that I wrote the book, which is, I believe, the first bridge to be built between the two territories.

MB. I opened it and dived headlong into your exponential curves, but in spite of my memories of matriculation, I threw in the sponge: I remained shrouded in the gloom of Plato's cavern: could an average intelligence understand your book?

X. Yes.

MB. Then I must be well below average!

X. A boy who has passed "Elementary Maths" at the lycée could easily take it in today: ten years ago, no.

MB. You have never made use of the serial system?

X. A little in METASTASEIS—that was its fault: it was because of this that the serialists criticized me, as being impure.

MB. Have you never since used it "systematically"?

X. No. Aesthetically and stylistically, serialism doesn't appeal to me; I haven't got that kind of sensibility which is Central European. Moreover, the serial system is only one particular case, and its possibilities are very slender when I compare them with those I meet in my own field. With the serial system one cannot, for example, encompass systems with glissandi, or continuous evolutions, or complexes more or less dense. In fact, it constitutes a particular case of the overall "massing" conception which I introduced in METASTASEIS.

MB. It is said that you have had a decisive influence on the younger Polish contemporary school whose aesthetic is close to your own. Even the not-so-young, such as Serocki or Lutoslawski came to a major turning point around 1960–61. In 1958 Lutoslawski was writing his "Funeral Music" à la Bartok, then in 1963 he wrote his "Three Poems of Henri Michaux", which was considered to be avante-garde. Serocki wrote a neo-classical Sinfonietta in 1956, then in 1963 his "Episodes" for strings and three percussion groups. When did you first go to Warsaw?

X. In 1962, when the turning point had already come.

MB. Did they know your works?

X. Certainly, I was received like an old acquaintance. METASTASEIS and PITHOPRAKTA had been broadcast on the German radio stations since 1957. In 1961 people coming back from Donaueschingen told me "You have a pupil in Poland: Penderecki".

MB. Do you know his music?

X. Yes, I was a member of the jury at the Biennale of the Museum of Modern Art in 1960. The score submitted by Penderecki was still in the vein of the Darmstadt serialists. I preferred a score for orchestra by Gorecki, with its sustained sounds, its masses, much more advanced. PITHO-PRAKTA had its first performance in an atmosphere of scandal in March 1957. This was the first work based on the calculus of probabilities and massed structures. The Swedish performance of METASTASEIS at that time also produced a reaction in Poland.

MB. Maurice Le Roux at the last Royan Festival told the story (in the presence of Penderecki and Markowski) of how, when he was invited to conduct in Warsaw three years previously, he had thought to himself when building his programme: "I am going to give them something quite new: PITHOPRAKTA". He received the following reply: "This work is already in our regular repertory"! Do these Polish composers make use of mathematics like yourself?

X. By no means, and more's the pity. They are concerned with the exterior aspect of the thing, of sound in itself and in its effects, like a kind of collage; I regret this because they can't go far along this road. I am glad that this sensibility for sounds has reached and captured the public; but on the other hand, as touching the basic matter, the construction on reasoning (which alone permits a large step forward), there is not a great deal I believe among the young Polish composers at present. However, I have faith in them; there is in Poland a school of mathematics that is absolutely first-rate.

MB. Their music is frequently classified as "tachist". Is your music "tachist"?

X. When one passes on from an isolated, individual phenomenon to a phenomenon produced en masse, as for example with string pizzicatos, one has a "cloud", a "galaxy" of pointed sounds: this galaxy is like a splodge. If you stay within the macrocosm, then it remains as tachism (all music is a kind of tachism), but if you cause this splodge to evolve, if you articulate the splodges, from that moment begins true music. Without that one if left with decorative music, one falls back on all that was done immediately after J. S. Bach.

MB. Have you been influenced in any way by any of the composers of the 20th Century?

X. Messiaen certainly; this can't strictly be called an influence because I don't think that any music I have composed at all resembles his, but he opened my eyes to a large extent. There was also the powerful influence of Scherchen's personality.

MB. But he wasn't a composer.

X. But what a widely cultured man! What an artist! Bartok also left an imprint on my early works. I remember around 1948 there was a concert given in Paris by Menuhin with Louis Kentner at the piano. The audience booed. I had never heard this music before and I was shattered by it.

MB. Did you know that you were a figurehead, and that several young musicians have said to me: "my two masters are Messiaen and Xenakis"?

X. Come now, mastery is . . .

MB. Do you have any desire to mould the young?

X. No, what interests me are personal contacts. The Japanese Takahashi, for instance. I heard him in Japan and was impressed by him. As a pianist, since he was passionate about the music I was writing, he wanted to know how it was made, so I wrote to him: "learn mathematics", and I gave him the names of a few books. He learnt it. He then commissioned a work for piano: thus I wrote HERMA for him. Later Takahashi asked to come and live near me. I told him that I didn't give lessons, but he was welcome to live near at hand. With my Ford grant I took him to Berlin, then introduced him to Paris. Meanwhile he had learnt French; he had mastered "programming" and now knew as much as I did—he even made corrections to my book, "Musiques Formelles". He uncovered several mathematical errors. He made a "programme" on his own, though I don't yet know with what result. The relations I have with him are that on the level of sensibility and of conception we are very close together, and I greatly admire his piano-playing and his general attitude towards music.

MB. Which composers do you esteem?

X. Well, the Poles; I value their fearlessness: it is admirable to hurl oneself like that in a totally new direction: they have risked much, and I think they will benefit from it. I have esteem for Boulez, not so much for his orchestral works, but more for his piano works and his quartet—certain parts of his quartet. And Messiaen, obviously, for example his Livre d'Orgue and his Catalogue d'Oiseaux. Amy shows a certain serious orthodoxy, which could develop along a more original path. I think that he has the fibre of an artist and that he is about to transform himself into an interesting personality. I esteem Schaeffer for what he does. Philippot—there is a poet; I met him in '58 and we immediately discovered close affinities: he was the only one I could talk to; he knew mathematics and had very wide interests, not just as a musician. We joined forces for about 2 or 3 years. We even founded a kind of group with Alain de Chambure, a technician and man of very rare intelligence, and Molles. Then Philippot took a high executive post. I often said to him: "drop these posts and return to your true métier".

MB. And the other avant-garde artists?

X. I know few of them. I'm too busy working on my own account. Perhaps I'm wrong. I don't much care for present-day painting. We won't mention Pop art or Op art, which are a debased form. What counts is that I sometimes recognize among them interesting characters, worthwhile personalities. I reckon that nature, its micro-organisms that one can now photograph on an enormous scale, represent realms of sensibility, of the same order, but much stronger, more advanced. There is a confusion, a cacophony in the realm of thought of painting of today; one doesn't know where it is going, it seems to be in gestation.

MB. And advanced poetry?

X. I am not very well versed in it. Poetry seems to me to be undergoing a struggle between its origin, which is the expression by words, and the music of words, its sonority; and I get the impression that it doesn't know which foot to stand on.

MB. The titles of your works are usually Greek words, expressing abstract notions.

X. EONTA, that is the neuter plural of the present participle of the verb "to be", that is to say "Beings": it is in the Ionian dialect of ancient philosophy (especially of Parmenides), EONTA is a kind of hommage to Parmenides. PITHOPRAKTA means "an act, action by probabilities. It is a portmanteau word. METASTASEIS is also a portmanteau word, it means "after the standstill", a dialectic idea of movement, that is continuity and discontinuity; this is the first time that I have worked with glissandi en masse. Glissandi existed before, but isolated, as a prolongation of a portamento; here for the first time they were in continuity, in movement. AKRATA means "pure", in the neuter plural. I must admit that I was also rather taken by the sonority of these words. They sound good, don't they? HERMA means "embryo, union, foundations", because this was the first time that I made use of logic calculus, of symbolic logic. NOMOS means "rules, laws", and also in music "a special or particular melody", occasionally also "mode". It is a word of the 6th or 7th Century before Christ, which is important musically. MORSIMA-AMORSIMA: "moros" is fate, death, destiny. "Morsima" is what comes about by fate. "A-" is a negative particle. "Amorsima" is that which does not come about by fate. Today the calculus of probabilities, the theory of large numbers, with the problems of choice, causality, of determinism, connect and clarify the ancient idea of Fate.

MB. Do your works always bear a direct relationship to your titles?

X. Yes, I try to sum up in a nutshell the idea which has dominated the work I have been doing, the kernel of the thought which I have put into the work.

MB. And the titles ST/4-0261, ST/10 and ST/48 . . .

X. For stochastic music these are generic to the passage of the works through the machine. They are quite simple: ST indicates stochastic music, 4 for 4 instruments, 0261 calculated in February of the year 1961.

MB. You are well versed in the philosophies of ancient Greece, of the theatre, literature, architecture, in fact of the whole of the ancient Greek civilisation.

X. My youth was saturated with it.

MB. Do you remain faithful to it?

X. Yes, because I am always rediscovering in the civilisation of ancient Greece the germ of the most advanced ideas of contemporary life.

MB. And Greek myths? as resuscitated in the 20th Century?—and all these Antigones, Orpheuses, Oedipuses brought up to date?

X. I find these counterfeits deplorable.

MB. All the same, thank heaven that Racine counterfeited Phaedra.

X. What's the use? An artist must express his own epoch; the subjects themselves must be new. Look at Brecht: we don't take into account enough that there is a modern mythology.

MB. AKRATA is quite new, 11 minutes of chamber music.

X. This is an introduction in the extra-temporal category of music (which is extra-temporal thought); it is a sketch in which I make use of the theory of Groups. This theory, of immense importance, concerns those objects or abstract figures which bear a certain relation to each other: for example, in arithmetic, an addition is made of natural numbers, which are the group elements, their addition gives another group element of the same nature. Nought is a neutral element since it doesn't alter anything if you add it to an element. You have inverses—these are negatives. In geometry let's take the polygon: a group will be born by the rotary movement of this polygon around an axis or around one of the apexes. With a triangle you only have three possibilities in the relationship of one apex to the other two, and, as with the polygon, the group will be of a cyclical nature, limited, closed. But with numbers the group is infinite. In music there are all kinds of things one can discover and make use of to enclose them within the rules of this internal logic. Going one step further, in AKRATA I have used "imaginary" numbers.

MB. And NOMOS for 'cello solo?

X. This is an even deeper exploration into the structure of groups and extra-temporal structures. The outside-time is static. It is a construction of the spirit, while the temporal is the happening, the materiality of fact.

MB. POLLA TA DHINA for a small ensemble of children who chant the same note over an accompaniment for reduced orchestra . . .

X. . . . was written for the Stuttgart Festival of Light Music (!) The text is taken from the Antigone of Sophocles; it is the one text that speaks of Man, it is a hymn to Man: the finest of the wonders of the world is Man. It is an oasis in this formidable tragedy.

MB. What work have you on the stocks?

X. The Ministry of Cultural Affairs offered me a commission. I refused the money for the commission as a protest against its indignity: 3000 francs, which I returned to sender. But I was already writing the work and I gave it for nothing. The commission was received very late in

October 1965 and the work has to have its first performance at the Royan Festival at the beginning of April 1966; I therefore had 4 months in which to write it; but besides this, having previously undertaken this ORESTEIA for Ypsilanti which must be ready for May, I wanted to refuse Royan. However, Claude Samuel who runs this festival, insisted, since Scherchen had just accepted to direct the first performance. The work is entitled TERRETEKTORH. It is written for large orchestra—Beethoven forces. The novelty will be that the musicians will be sprinkled among the audience, with the conductor at the centre on a circular rostrum. The idea of placing the orchestra in among the audience has preoccupied me for a long time. I have always been disagreeably physically uncomfortable when I have listened to music from a distance. I thought to myself: this is a beautiful instrument, why hear it from a distance where 50% of its life is lost? Then a memory struck me: I was standing on a rock in a storm, the rain, the waves, a frenetic gale came at me from all sides all at the same time (that's nature for you isn't it?). Thus there is a precedent for TERRETEKTORH. LES SUPPLIANTES was a work which I wrote for Epidaurus, in which I armed the 40 girls in the chorus with percussion instruments: little bells and castanets (copied from a specimen which I found in a German museum), which accompanied the dancing and singing. That was a new idea.

MB. Didn't they do that in the ancient theatre?

X. It is not known for certain. It is not impossible that the dancers had necklaces with jingles for instance, or on their arms. We don't know much about the ancient instruments. I know that they danced with rattles or with castanets. The other novelty in TERRETEKTORH is that I require each musician to play, besides his own normal instrument, four other elementary instruments: a wood-block, the clattering of which in large numbers is evocative of hail, a siren whistle (an example of which I found in a jazz music shop in Montmartre), whose massed blowing produces veritable flames of sound, and finally a maracas and a whip, whose mutterings and snappings could evoke whatever you like. It is evident that the large number of these instruments (90 of each) will give a galaxy of sounds sprinkled in space, that I have been searching for over the past 10 years. These instruments were chosen for their dry articulation and their impact of shock; the orchestral colour thus produced is altogether different from the pseudo-exotic climate of vibraphones, marimbaphones and other "phones" to which the scores of the avant-garde perpetually have recourse. Finally, a further reason for this scattering of musicians among the crowd is psychological. One is among them, speaks to them, turns the pages for them, one sees them working at close quarters. On their side, they get given initiative, a new scope, they are handling different instruments from their own—they are "playing".

MB. Your idea of scattering the sound among the public and the public among the music seems to me of great interest. To hear, chained to one's seat in a corner of a normal concert hall, an orchestra perched up on the stage is like looking at country view in the form of a picture postcard.

X. In fact, when Goléa stated at Royan: "I was sitting, quite by chance near a trombone; at the next performance of TERREKEKTORH if I am put near a violin I shall be hearing a completely different work", Jacques Bourgeois replied with good reason that he could see nothing extraordinary in that, and that one admires a view of the countryside from only one point of view at a time. A chance route brings you to a certain spot, and you enjoy the countryside just as it is presented to you at that moment.

MB. Aren't we ourselves scattered on the earth, falling from heaven like rain-drops to pursue our tiny course on earth, making do with what we are given, our nature, our faculties, and with those we meet? But that's philosophy . . .

X. Quite right. Of what use is our brain except to synthesize the different elements we meet with? You spend your time collecting little bits of an enormous puzzle which each person fits together in his own way. I wonder if one ought to hear even the classical works from a distance, as one normally does. So much is going on within the classical orchestra. One shouldn't apply this system in every case. A splitting up of the sections of the orchestra, studied according to each section, would surely alter the pleasure and way of thinking of the musician. In TERRETEKTORH one could imagine the public milling around among the musicians who could be perched up on little individual rostra, but it would be necessary to design a new architecture for concert halls to allow an all-round view from every angle. For the present one could perform TERRETEK-TORH in certain churches for example. After the first performance at Royan I went to the Philippines for an international congress on musicology (neither Boulez nor Cage, who were invited, could go). Afterwards I went on to the U.S.A. to do the stage music (an hour and a half of it) for Aeschylus' ORESTEIA which the town of Ypsilanti had commissioned for their Greek Theatre. Simonovic will direct it. In this also but with only 15 instruments, I am aiming at mobility of the music which will be interlocked with the stage action. I shall make the dancers play instruments.

MB. I have just seen a film on Varèse in the series "Great Rehearsals" realized by the research group of the O.R.T.F. Maderna was conducting: he is somewhat like Orson Welles; he works on the sound joyfully, like a sculptor pounding his clay. You yourself introduced the film and summed up at the end. Do you consider Varèse to be one of your masters? Is there any line leading from Varèse to you?

X. I like Varèse; I have the greatest admiration for the musician and the man, for his asceticism, his act of renunciation vis-à-vis music; with the tragedy of his life, and the fact that he "missed the bus" as the saying goes. But I am not really close to Varèse from the musical point of view. He practically never uses strings except in "Arcanes" which is an early work. Furthermore he has always been opposed to pre-established work, to systems and to all forms of structure; all that used to irritate him. His music didn't come to him that way. The first person to speak to me about him was Messiaen: in 1950 we were walking together near the Gare St. Lazare, and he said to me: "he is an exceptional person, perhaps the greatest composer of today, is Varèse". The second to speak of him was Le Corbusier. Then, in 1953, I heard some recorded works; there was his discovery of musique concrète, but besides this what he did with the normal instruments of the orchestra was for me like a flash of lightning. I can't say that I have been influenced by him, not consciously at any rate; I have never studied one of his scores, but I consider his creative thought as pure and as interesting as any other that I can think of.

MB. The young composer, J. P. Guézec (who likes to say "I have two masters, Messiaen and Xenakis") has recently written a "Suite Mondrian". Today Mondrian is "in"—even in the domain of haute-couture. The reason I mention this painter is because it seems to me his aesthetic pre-occupations during the years 1912–1920 often remind me of your own. At the core of the De Stijl movement, in which, among others, several architects collaborated (Oud, Wilson, van Eesteren, for whom "there was no essential difference between architecture and every other, form of creative enterprise") it is said that Mondrian, deeply involved with philosophy, and basing his aesthetics on philosophical ideas, posed a "neo-platonic system" which he called "positive mysticism" or "plastic mathematics", which led him to the conclusion that "art becomes a medium as exact as mathematics for representing the fundamental characteristics of the cosmos". Are you acquainted with these ideas?

X. There is no doubt that your comparison is of value. You see, all paintings, music, all the works of every age meet at some point. One is continually discovering parallels to a greater or lesser degree, confirmations, common sensibilities, and Mondrian had his share in the universal patrimony which one can in fact study in this way. I am less acquainted with Mondrian than I am with Klee, of whom I have seen a good deal in Paris, Munich and Zurich, and Malevitch (who preceded Mondrian a little); they seem to me to be the two absolute purists of modern painting. Malevitch, who was a much brighter and more logical spirit than Mondrian, had established what he called the "aesthetic theories of the moment", whose standpoint is most interesting. I came across the painting of Mondrian quite by chance in 1959 with Philippot. For our conferences we worked by "grids": all our subjects for consideration were set down in double entry tables of lines and columns. We were trying to find a way of illustrating our calculations: it was thus that we noticed the role played by the grid in regard to Klee's and Mondrian's concept of painting, and similarly in all kinds of sciences and human expressions.

MB. We have had a good walk round you. Can we now enter into your personal life? Your wife, who lived through the occupation in France, has received several notable decorations.

X. When she was 13.

MB. What for?

X. She saved a number of lives. She was in the true resistance.

MB. And she is about to publish her third novel. What do you think of it?

X. It is compact, warm and lively. She knows how to write; she is original.

MB. You mentioned to me that you yourself took part in the anti-Nazi resistance.

X. In Greece from 1940 to January '45. But in that country it was the Resistance that lost.

MB. Your face-wound?

X. 1st January 1945.

MB. Some people have told me that in Greece you are a national hero—did you know it?

X. . . .

MB. Coming to France in '47 you turned over a new leaf?

X. I closed up a book. I drew a line through all that very intense part of my life which had lasted for 7 years, from '40 to '47: this was a great step to take at the age I was then. One had to make a choice, that sorrowful choice of which Valéry speaks in "The Architect". I chose music— France and music. I had lost much time, and much hope as well.

MB. When someone spoke of your "de-sensitized, de-humanized art", were they aware of how much human fervour there was in your adolescence and that this kind of fire burnt for 7 years?

X. A large part of my music has its roots in this period. My wife says that my music is of the war. Before 1940 my life as a student was quite different—it was classicism, antiquity, philosophy, poetry. I always went around with a Plato in my pocket: then I read Marx, which is partial platonism, but with more realism. But Marx was only a thinker: Lenin was greater: a philosopher, sociologist, demagogue, aesthete, leader all at the same time, the sum of which constitutes a statesman of rare stature.

MB. The evolution of your life, your intellectual youth, the violence of the war years, then isolation, choice of a difficult path, and now success (you appear in this year's edition of Larousse!) does that seem normal to you?

X. I don't know by what process of determinism this was all brought about. I only know that I almost lost my life, that I almost failed to achieve anything, that those trials have made me what I am, and that all that is as it should be. Greeks are like that: they are a people continually in search of themselves, always ready to launch out into all kinds of rapid, violent, sometimes fatal actions, and end up by not finding themselves.

MB. "A Greek race a kingly race, a race without hope" wrote Paul Eluard. Are you happy to be a composer of music?

X. Not often. You have no idea of the anguish that that betokens, the difficulty of making, of abandoning, something of one's self, to be judged and to be incapable of judging oneself, incapable of knowing what one is. "For one more or less free bar, there are twenty which suffocate under the weight of a tradition, whose hypocritical and base influence, in spite of my efforts, I keep encountering", wrote Debussy in 1911.

OPINIONS AND COMMENTS

HERMANN SCHERCHEN

A musician of deep perceptions, a pure spirit and one imbued with the creative fire. I expect from him works of art expressing new human capacities.

LEONARD BERNSTEIN

It was a great pleasure and a privilege for me to conduct PITHOPRAKTA.

AARON COPLAND

Xenakis is, in my opinion, the possessor of a special and original kind of composition. There is a curious fascination in each thing he writes, and I look forward to each new work with great interest.

HENRY BARRAUD

A great artistic temperament, a prodigious imagination, exceptional creative gifts.

CLAUDE ROSTAND

". . . Are Machaut's 'Mass', Beethoven's 'Great Fugue' or 'The Rite of Spring' easy on the ear"? Provided with a considerable general culture and armed with the more specialised equipment of the musician, the mathematician and the architect, Iannis Xenakis has shown, from the beginning of his young career, that he meant to cultivate music on a somewhat larger scale than just as an art to give pleasure. It was to show at the same time that he was trying to give to this form of human expression its full dimensions by means of new techniques and æsthetics of his own time and in the perspective of his own time. . . . What is certain is that the almost unanimous critical opinion of today, even among the more conservative section, grants Xenakis a "felicity" and an indisputable musical gift. One likes or dislikes it, but one admits that the music is there. Olivier Messiaen's epitome expresses this best: "The astonishing thing," he writes, "is that the preliminary calculations are forgotten in performance. Nothing cerebral, no intellectual frenzy, the resulting sound is a stirring excitement that may be either delicately poetic or violently brutal, according to the case. . . ."

OLIVIER MESSIAEN

(Reprint of the text of Messiaen's introduction to the "Festival Xenakis" concert on 20th May, 1965, at the Salle Gaveau, Paris.)

I have been asked to introduce the concert devoted to the works of Iannis Xenakis. If the reader of this introduction would like to join me in glancing at the programme of the concert, he will find therein several strange titles which will persuade him from the outset that this concerns a kind of music, a musician and a man of no ordinary stamp.

Here, first of all, is EONTA. Eonta=being. This term is applied to the fact itself of existence in the Ionian philosophy (example: Parmenides, whose theories profess the continuity of being). It concerns a work for brass and piano that is entirely new in its sonorities and in its conceptions of time, of which the least one could say is that in fact it exists, and with a surprising force of existence. Here again is ATREES. One thinks immediately of the Atrides—and when one learns that this work is dedicated to Blaise Pascal (who was not only a great Christian and illustrious author of the "Pensées", but also a physician and mathematician of genius and discoverer of the calculus of probabilities), one instinctively brings together the two ideas of *fatality and chance*. And one discovers at the same time the key to the world of Xenakis in knowing that *chance is calculated*. Now, the calculus of the aleatoric, called by Xenakis the "Stochastic" (indicated by the letters ST in the first work on the programme) is precisely the summing up of Xenakis' approach and the explanation of that *crossing from mathematics to music* which has caused his name to be surrounded with so much clamour.

In the last work mentioned in the programme, ACHORRIPSIS, we find bodies of held notes, bodies of pizzicati, bodies of glissandi. These bodies, these masses, these crowds (which Xenakis himself compares with certain natural global events in sound, such as the myriad little shocks produced by rain-drops on a hard surface) cannot be apprehended directly by the musician. Let us take several simultaneously played glissandi having the same duration but of different range— or, vice versa, several simultaneous glissandi having the same range but of different durations— in both cases all the speeds of the gliding from note to note will be different, and the meeting together of the sounds will be of an indiscernible complexity. Analogous phenomena will result by using masses of held notes and clouds of pizzicati. The calculus of probabilities (whether assisted or not by an electronic brain) will allow a more certain foreseeing of most of these details. This is the work of Xenakis: architect—mathematician—logician . . . also poet and musician . . . a man of no ordinary stamp.

PROFESSOR G. TH. GUILBAUD, mathematician and director of studies of the department of Social Mathematics and Statistics at the Ecole Pratique des Hautes Etudes, Paris. (reprint of the note on "Les Recherches Musicales" of 29th April 1965)

I have followed, for several years past, some of the studies and musical creations undertaken by I. Xenakis. He himself has joined in many of our working gatherings at the Centre de Mathématique Sociale. An initial dialogue has thus been formed which allows me—apart from the esteem which I have for the scientific and artistic qualities of I. Xenakis—to appreciate his projects for further research.

The exploitation of electronic resources, present or future, seems to me to be an inevitable path, as much to give substance to methodical reflections on musical creation as to stimulate these reflections themselves: already in several fields of mathematical research such co-operation has born fruit, and others are in the process of development.

The problem of marrying sound-producing instruments with the mechanisms of composition is beyond my competence; I wish that technicians with minds open to argument would interest themselves in it, and a few preliminary soundings have persuaded me that this should be possible. In any case, each step taken along this path will render considerable service to another branch of researches that is of most interest to me professionally, which is linked to those that are leading us into various regions of the scientific study of human activities.

Not only could music (considered as a social activity) benefit by the application of mathematics, in all its present-day extensions, but, in return, the adoption by mathematics of the "human sciences" could be strongly stimulated by the progress of such musical studies as those conceived by Iannis Xenakis. I am therefore ready to witness the interest of those who could help the realisation of such projects in one manner or another; and I am also ready to collaborate therein and to enlist those questing spirits among my entourage who should be tempted by this adventure.

SCHIN-ICHI MAJSUSHITO, Tokyo

. . . But what is the most remarkable thing of all is the dynamism of Xenakis' works, and the energetic intensity that surges up at the intersections of ascending and descending glissandi. No one could doubt his unique originality.

BOHDAN POCIEJ, Warsaw

PITHOPRAKTA functions like a cataract, a current of condensed expression; the action is powerful and clear, flowing in a single direction. That the motive force which underlies the work of Xenakis is becoming more and more powerful and universal is proved by the latest works of Stockhausen, and also by the most recent productions of the Polish avant-garde.

CHRONOLOGICAL LIST OF WORKS

WORKS FOR ORCHESTRA

METASTASEIS for orchestra of 61 players (1953–54)

Instrumentation: Piccolo, Flute, 2 Oboes, Bass Clarinet, 3 Horns, 2 Trumpets, 2 Tenor Trombones, Timpani, Percussion and Strings (12, 12, 8, 8, 6).

Duration: 8 minutes.

Dedicated to Maurice Le Roux.

First performance: 1955. Donaueschingen Festival.
Conductor, Hans Rosbaud.

Publisher: Boosey & Hawkes.

Explanation of the title: Meta=after+stasis=a state of standstill=dialectic transformation. The *metastases* are a hinge between classical music (which includes serial music) and "formalized" music which the composer was obliged to inculcate into composition. Here are a few new ideas introduced by this work:

(1) The normal orchestra is totally divisi: 61 instrumentalists play 61 different parts, thus introducing the mass conception in music (music built with a large number of sound events).

(2) Systematic use of individual glissandi throughout the whole mass of orchestral strings; glissandi whose gradients are calculated individually. These glissandi create sound spaces in continuous evolution, comparable to ruled surfaces and volumes. It was precisely these glissandi which led the composer several years later to the architectural conception of the Philips pavilion at the 1958 Brussels Exposition, on behalf of Le Corbusier. (Cf. Le Poème Electronique, Editions de Minuit and Revue Technique Philips, Vol. 20 (1958–59).

(3) Intervallic structures, duration of dynamics and of timbres are combined in calling upon geometrical progressions, in particular those of the golden mean, conceptions analagous to those applied by the composer in designing the façades of the Convent of La Tourette near Lyon. (Cf. Modulor 2, Le Corbusier, Editions Architecture d'Aujourd'hui.)

(4) The putting into correlation according to "rank" the characters of sonorous events, first step towards the calculus of probabilities.

(5) It was also an attempt to demonstrate at that time that the human orchestra was capable of out-classing, in the matter of new sonorites and in finesse, the new electro-magnetic techniques which were threatening to oust them.

PITHOPRAKTA for orchestra of 50 instruments (1955–56)

Instrumentation: 2 Tenor Trombones, Xylophone, Wood-block, Strings (12, 12, 8, 8, 6).

Duration: 10 minutes.

Dedicated to Hermann Scherchen.

First performance: 8th March, 1957. Musica Viva Concerts, Munich. Conductor, Hermann Scherchen.

Publisher: Boosey & Hawkes.

Explanation of title: Pithoprakta=actions by probabilities. The composer, in making use of information derived from the calculus of probabilities, is seeking here a confrontation of continuity and discontinuity by glissandi and pizzicati, by tappings with the bow *col legno* or by very short touches of the bow *naturale*, also by striking with the hand the backs of the instruments, which, in the case of the strings, are all divisi.

It is an approach to stochastic (probabilist) music. With the glissandi, which could perhaps be likened to straight lines, sonorous volumes are generated. With a large quantity of "pointed" sounds, propagated throughout the entire breadth of the sound-spectrum, there appears a dense "granulation", a veritable cloud of sonorous material in movement, regulated by the laws of large numbers (Laplace-Gauss, Maxwell-Boltzmann, Poisson, Pearson, Fisher). Thus the individual sound loses its own importance for the gain of the ensemble, looked at en bloc, in its totality. The ambition of the composer is, then, to discover a new "morphology" of sound, that will be stirring both by means of its abstract aspect (probabilist theory) as of its concrete one (the aural sensation of its extraordinary sounds). Cf. Gravesaner Blätter Nos. 1 & 6 Gravesano, Ticino, Switzerland, also Musiques Formelles, ed. Richard-Masse, 7 Place St. Sulpice, Paris VIe.

ACHORRIPSIS for 21 instruments (1956–57)

Instrumentation: Piccolo, Oboe, Clarinet in E♭, Bass Clarinet, Bassoon, Contrabassoon, 2 Trumpets, Tenor Trombone, Xylophone, Wood-block, Bass Drum, 3 Violins, 3 Violoncellos, 3 Doublebasses.

Duration: 7 minutes.

First performance: 1958. Buenos Aires. Conductor, Herman Scherchen.

Publisher: Böte und Bock, Berlin.

Explanation of the title: Jets of sound. There exists within a given space musical instruments and men; there is no cause or will ordained to produce the sounds. But in a sufficiently long period of time, it is probable that there will come by chance a generation of certain sounds having certain durations, certain spectra, certain speeds etc. . . . These rare sonorous events could be other than just isolated sounds. They could perhaps be either melodic figures, or cellular structures or agglomerations whose characteristics are equally ruled by the laws of chance, for example: the clouds of "pointed" sounds, the temperatures of speeds, etc. . . . In all ways they form a sample of a chain succession of sonorous events. ACHORRIPSIS constitutes a sample of aleatoric disturbances organised with the help of the calculus of probabilities. Its morphology is based on Poisson's Law and is worked out with the aid of a matrix, prototype of this compositional stochastic behaviour. Cf. Gravesaner Blätter No. 11/12 Gravesano, Ticino, Switzerland, and Musiques Formelles, ed. Richard-Masse, Paris.

ST/10 for 10 instruments (1956–62)

Instrumentation: Clarinet, Bass Clarinet, 2 Horns, Harp, Percussion (5 temple-blocks, 4 tom-toms, 2 congas, wood-block), String Quartet (or String Orchestra).

Duration: 12 minutes.

Dedicated to Konstantin Simonovic and L'Ensemble Instrumental, de Musique Contemporaine de Paris.

First performance: 1962. At the IBM, Place Vendôme, Paris. Conductor, K. Simonovic.

Publisher: Boosey & Hawkes.

Explanation of the title: as shown by its components: ST/10—1,080262. ST=stochastic music. Stochastic in mathematics means: aleatoric, by chance, according to probabilities, and was introduced by Jacques Bernoulli; 10=10 instruments; 1=the first work for this number of players; 080262=8th of February 1962, the date on which this work was calculated by the electronic brain. ST/10 was calculated by the 7090 IBM electronic brain in Paris in obedience to a special stochastic (probabilist) "programme" devised by Xenakis. This "programme" was derived from the thesis of "Minimum of Rules of Composition", which had already been formulated in ACHORRIPSIS, but it was not until several years later that it became possible to have it "mechanised" at IBM-France.

The "programme" is a complex of stochastic laws which the composer had been introducing into musical composition for a number of years. He orders the electronic brain to define all the sounds of a sequence, previously calculated, one after the other. First, the time of its occurrence, next its class of timbre (arco, pizzicato, glissando, etc.), its instrument, its pitch, the gradient of its glissando where that occurs, the duration and dynamic of the emission of the sound. Cf. Musiques

Formelles, ed. Richard-Masse, Paris, and for the full programme in Fortran language see Gravesaner Blätter No. 26, Gravesano, Ticino, Switzerland.

AMORSIMA—MORSIMA for 10 players (1956–62)

Instrumentation: Clarinet, Bass Clarinet, 2 Horns, Harp. Percussion (5 temple-blocks, 4 tom-toms, 2 congas, wood-block) String Quartet.

Duration: 5 minutes.

First performance: 1962. Athens. Conductor, Lukas Foss.

Publisher: Boosey & Hawkes.

Explanation of the title: Moros=fate, death. Morsima=that which comes by fate. Amorsima (*a* being the negative particle)=that which does not come by fate. This work results from exploiting the same "programme" as ST/10 (see above).

DUEL—Game for Two Orchestras (1959)

Instrumentation: 2 Piccolos, 2 Oboes, 2 Clarinets in B♭, 2 Clarinets in E♭, 2 Bass Clarinets, 2 Bassoons, 2 Contrabassoons, 4 Trumpets, 2 Trombones, Percussion (2 Snare-drums, 2 Side-drums, 4 Bongos, 6 Congas) and Strings (2,2,0,8,4).

Duration: Between 10 and 30 minutes according to the outcome of the game.

Publisher: Boosey & Hawkes.

Commissioned by O.R.T.F., Paris. DUEL is a musical game played by the two conductors of the two orchestras, resulting in a winner and a loser, analogous to the game STRATEGIE (see below).

SYRMOS for 18 Strings (1959)

Instrumentation: 6 Violin I, 6 Violin II, 3 Violoncellos, 3 Doublebasses.

Duration: 15 minutes.

Dedicated to Hermann Scherchen.

First performance: 20th May 1965. At the Festival of Xenakis' works in Paris.
Conductor, K. Simonovic.

Publisher: Boosey & Hawkes.

Explanation of the title: Chain succession, train of events. The work is based on stochastic transformations of eight basic textures:

(a) strands of horizontal parallel lines

(b) strands of ascending parallel lines (glissandi)

(c) strands of descending parallel lines (glissandi)

(d) networks of crossing parallel lines (ascending and descending)

(e) clouds of pizzicati

(f) atmospheres of *col legno* taps with short *col legno* glissandi

(g) configurations of glissandi treated as ruled surfaces

(h) geometric configurations of converging or diverging glissandi.

The mathematical structure of this work is the same as that of "Analogique A" and "Analogique B" (see below: electronic works), that is to say based on Markovian stochastic processes. (See Musiques Formelles, chapter II, ed. Richard-Masse, 7 St. Sulpice, Paris VI).

ST/48 for 48 players (1959–62)

Instrumentation: Piccolo, Flute, 2 Oboes, Clarinet, Bass Clarinet, Bassoon, Contrabassoon, 2 Horns, 2 Trumpets, 2 Trombones, Timpani, Percussion (4 Tom-toms, 5 Temple-blocks, Wood-block, Side-drum, Vibraphone, Marimbaphone) and Strings (8,8,6,6,4).

Duration: 11 minutes.

Commissioned by O.R.T.F. (France-Inter) in 1961.

Publisher: Boosey & Hawkes.

Explanation of the title: as shown by its components: ST/48—1,240162 (see ST/10 above). This work was calculated by the 7090 IBM in Paris in obedience to a special stochastic (probabilist) "programme" devised by Xenakis. This "programme" was derived from the thesis of "Minimum of Rules in Composition which had already been formulated in ACHORRIPSIS, but it was not until several years later that it became possible to have it "mechanised" at IBM-France.

The "programme" is a complex of stochastic laws which the composer had been introducing into musical composition for a number of years. He orders the electronic brain to define all the sounds of a sequence, previously calculated, one after the other. First the time of its occurrence, next its class of timbre (arco, pizzicato, glissando, etc.), its instrument, its pitch, the gradient of its glissando where that occurs, the duration and dynamic of the emission of the sound. (Bibliography as for ST/10).

STRATEGIE Game for two orchestras (1959–62)

Instrumentation: 2 Piccolos, 2 Flutes, 2 Oboes, 2 Clarinets in B♭, 2 Clarinets in E♭, 2 Bass Clarinets, 2 Bassoons, 2 Contrabassoons, 4 Horns, 4 Trumpets, 4 Tenor Trombones, 2 Tubas, Percussion (2 Vibraphones, 2 Marimbaphones, 2 Maracas, 2 Suspended Cymbals, 2 Bass Drums, 2×4 Tom-toms, 2×5 Temple-blocks, 2×4 Wood-blocks, 2×5 Goat-bells) and Strings (12,12,8,8,6).

Duration: 10 to 30 minutes, according to the outcome of the game.

First performance: 1963. Venice Festival. Conductors, Bruno Maderna and K. Simonovic.

Publisher: Boosey & Hawkes.

*Rules of the Game

STRATEGIE, dedicated to Mario Labroca, composed in 1962 and first performed in 1963 at the Venice Festival, when it was conducted by B. Maderna and K. Simonovic (Maderna was the winner), is the second "model" of one family of works of which the prototype was DUEL, also for 2 conductors and 2 orchestras, commissioned by the O.R.T.F. and composed in 1959.

Two orchestras are placed to left and right of the platform, with the two conductors back to back, or on two rostra placed diametrically opposite each other. They select and play one of six sound-structures numbered in the score from 1 to 6 that we shall call "tactics". These are of stochastic (probabilist) structure, and have been calculated by the 7090 IBM in Paris. Besides these six fundamental "tactics" each conductor may make his orchestra play certain simultaneous combinations of the six "tactics", two or three at a time. Here is the list of the six fundamental "tactics":

I   Wind instruments
II   Normal percussion
III   Backs of the stringed instruments struck with the hand
IV   "Pointillisme" of the strings
V   Glissandi of strings
VI   Sustained string harmonics

And here is the list of the 13 possible simultaneous combinations of the basic "tactics" valid for each orchestra:

VII = 1+2	XII = 2+3	XVI = 1+2+3
VIII = 1+3	XIII = 2+4	XVII = 1+2+4
IX = 1+4	XIV = 2+5	XVIII = 1+2+5
X = 1+5	XV = 2+6	XIX = 1+2+6
XI = 1+6		

Therefore there are 19 "tactics" in all which each conductor may execute with his own orchestra. In consequence the two conductors between them can make 19×19, i.e. 361 possible simultaneous couplings.

Cf. my book Musiques Formelles Chapter III, ed. Richard-Masse, 7 Place St. Sulpice, Paris 6e

To each of these 361 combinations is given a positive or negative whole number, which represents, according to the composer's reckoning, the points (partial payments) which one of the conductors, whom we shall call X, gains or loses. These numbers are noted down in a double-entry table at the intersections of the 19 horizontal lines and the 19 vertical columns. The 19 horizontal lines represent the tactics possible for conductor X and the 19 vertical columns those of his adversary, whom we shall call Y. All the positive numbers will be gains for X and losses for Y, and similarly, since the game is a dual one, all the negative numbers gains for Y and losses for X. We shall call this table the "Matrix of the Game". The game has been mathematically tested as being fair to both sides.

The musical game of STRATEGIE then consists of the choice and execution by conductor X of one of the 19 tactic-lines, while the other conductor, Y, plays one of the tactic-columns and reciprocally while X plays one of the tactic-lines Y chooses and plays against him one of the 19 tactic-columns, and so on.

Thus the game appears as the execution of a succession of different couplings which result from the "tactics" played simultaneously by the two orchestras according to the choice effected by each conductor without interruption.

1. CHOICE OF TACTICS. How will the conductors choose which "tactics" to play?

They may choose them in different ways. Examples: in an arbitrary way, following their own intuition, without taking into account the Matrix of the Game, or by drawing each time one of the 19 cards of the game, or even by considering the result of drawing out of a hat slips of paper marked with numbers from 1 to 19, but in different proportions; or even by previously concerted plan, they may direct a fixed succession of tactics. Or again the direction of the two orchestras may be handed over to only one conductor, who may apply any of the preceding methods. In fact all these ways constitute what one may call "degenerate" conflicting situations. The only worthwhile way, the only way which adds something new, in the case of more than one orchestra, is that which is governed by gains and losses, by victories or defeats.

Thus, in the case of STRATEGIE, the conductors must follow the points (gains and losses) shown on the Matrix of the Game. For example, the conductor who begins with a tactic is counter-attacked by his opposing conductor with the help of one which will give him the maximum number of points. The former then attacks again with another tactic which will give *him* the maximum number of points, and so on. In practice each should be able to foresee what his adversary is likely to do several moves in advance in order, as in chess, to be able to choose the best succession of tactics.

Each conductor announces the next tactic to his orchestra in several ways, but he has technical means at his disposal shown on the plan. This announcement will be made with the aid of light-signals in four colours activated by a switch-box (see the plan on page 31).

2. LIMITS OF THE GAME. The game is limited in general in several ways:

(a) The conductors may fix in advance a definite number of "tricks": let us say "n" tricks. The one to gain the maximum number of points at the end of the nth trick is the winner.

(b) An upper limit of points may be fixed: the one to reach it first becomes the winner.

(c) They may settle on a total duration for the game, say "m" minutes (or seconds): the one who gains the highest score at the "m"th minute (or second) is the winner.

3. AWARDING OF POINTS. This may be done in two ways:

(a) To have an umpire who notes down the points in two columns: one for conductor X, in which he inscribes positive numbers, and the other for conductor Y, in which he inscribes negative numbers. It is up to the umpire to annouce the results to the public.

(b) Without an umpire, but having instead an automatic signalling system, which consists of an individual table for each conductor with "n" buttons corresponding to the tactics of the matrix used. These buttons are linked to signal tables placed near the different groups of the orchestra, also a simple adding machine which will tot up the results on an electric panel in such a way as to be visible to the public as the game proceeds, like the score-board in a sports stadium (see plan for signalling system on page 31).

4. APPORTIONING OF LINES (AND COLUMNS) may be done by the conductors tossing a coin.

5. DESIGNATION OF THE STARTER. The conductor who is to make the first gambit may be chosen by another toss of a coin.

6. READING OF THE TACTICS (SCORES). They are played cyclically in an enclosed loop. Thus the finish of a tactic is made instantaneously on a bar-line at the discretion of the conductor. The subsequent eventual resumption of this tactic can be made:

(a) either reckoning from the bar-line defined above.

(b) or reckoning from a bar-line at a letter which the conductor will indicate visually by displaying to the orchestra a large card from a pile of letter cards placed near him. With letter-cards ranging from A to U, the conductor has available 22 different points of entry for each one of his tactics.

The tactics in the score have durations of at least two minutes. On reaching the end of the tactic, the conductors begin again at the beginning of that tactic—from where the "da capo" is written in the scores. Tempi and other nuances are left to the choice of each conductor, within the limits indicated in the score.

7. DURATION OF GAMBITS. The duration of each gambit is optional. Nevertheless it is as well to define a lower limit of the order of 10 seconds; that is to say if a conductor embarks on a certain tactic, he must maintain it for at least 10 seconds. This 10 seconds may vary from concert to concert. It represents a wish on the part of the composer but not an obligation, and the conductors have the right to decide before the game the lower limit of each gambit. There is no upper limit because the game conditions the maintaining or changing of a tactic. The penalties for not respecting the conventions are arranged in advance by the two conductors.

8. RESULT OF THE CONTEST. To emphasize the dual structure of this composition, and to give some acknowledgement to the conductor who most faithfully follows the conditions imposed by the composer by means of the Matrix of the Game, one could allow at the end of the contest:—

(a) The announcement of the winner

(b) The presentation of a prize—a bouquet of flowers or a cup or a medal—that the concert promoter might care to donate.

9. IN CONCLUSION. The losing conductor should not necessarily be considered as less good than the winner. In this respect this musical (artistic) game differs radically by definition from athletic sports or card-games. The winner wins simply because he has more closely followed the rules of the game imposed by the composer, who in consequence reclaims the responsibility for what is "beautiful" or "ugly" in his music. The game of STRATEGIE is finally a superstructure overlaying stochastic structures conceived in such a way that no combination of opposing tactics should be ugly.

The general application of this idea would permit the active participation of the public, who, by a collective judgment could establish the Matrix of the Game; but this experiment has yet to be tried out. On the other hand, the bidding is open . . .

STRATEGIE
PLANS OF DISPOSITION AND SIGNALLING SYSTEM

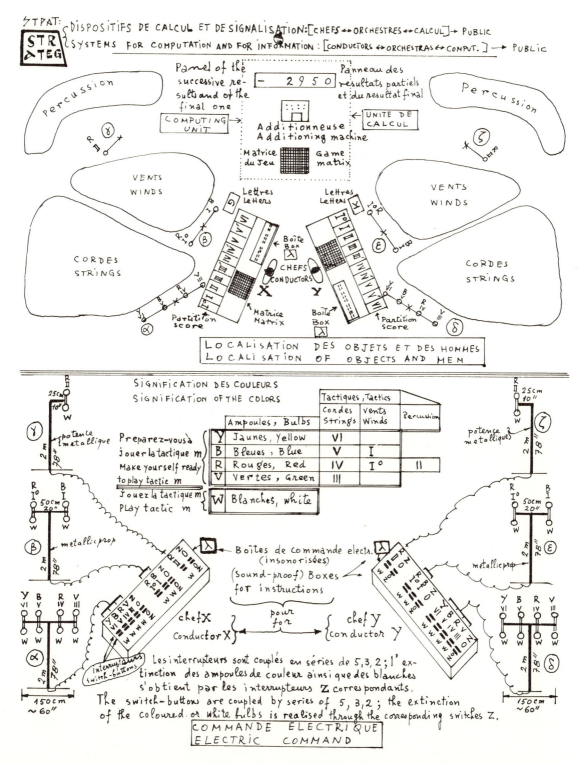

Localisation des objets et des hommes
Localisation of objects and men

Signification des couleurs
Signification of the colors

Commande électrique
Electric command

CHEF Y (colonnes)

	I	II	III	IV	V	VI	VII	VIII	IX	X	XI	XII	XIII	XIV	XV	XVI	XVII	XVIII	XIX	
I / I°	116	10	84	-48	4	-52	-60	-40	132	-44	-8	-36	-22	24	-46	102	138	-38	32	2
II	-56	96	-44	-22	-24	52	-50	-14	12	28	6	-48	-20	-16	-10	-24	-36	-20	44	3
III	-110	-2	96	96	24	0	4	-56	-32	-24	4	-52	-48	-40	-16	-44	-16	20	72	1
IV	0	-20	24	84	4	-12	12	-12	-28	8	-8	-24	-40	4	22	-10	-16	28	-16	11
V	-110	-204	-86	4	104	-8	44	20	-8	4	8	-8	-38	-24	-16	40	8	20	-24	1
VI	24	44	12	-14	-6	64	24	-8	24	4	-24	-40	-52	-44	24	44	4	4	-48	7
VII	-56	-52	20	16	36	44	44	4	-52	-48	0	-46	-36	-12	-20	-40	-44	16	40	4
VIII	-32	-8	-52	-8	12	4	4	48	-44	-12	8	-52	-4	8	32	-36	-40	-16	24	3
IX	-36	10	-16	-32	2	4	-44	-52	52	44	2	48	-18	64	24	22	-36	-28	-52	6
X	-48	22	-22	4	-4	32	-46	-16	8	-36	-24	-4	8	32	24	4	-8	20	-32	4
XI	4	24	26	-4	4	-28	-36	-12	20	4	64	68	4	40	-12	-2	-24	-27	-32	10
XII	-36	-196	-188	-28	-34	-42	36	32	24	0	-32	74	76	-4	4	-32	-28	40	76	7
XIII	166	-20	-42	-40	-52	-44	14	-16	4	22	-14	80	72	-26	-58	40	-18	78	42	2
XIV	32	-14	-34	0	-32	-52	36	12	-12	36	24	-28	42	76	-48	-64	-30	-29	72	5
XV	-20	8	4	28	-28	14	0	20	2	-4	-32	14	26	-56	46	-36	12	-8	14	4
XVI	88	88	104	-28	20	16	-2	-16	20	-20	-50	-26	-8	-36	-40	108	-24	-33	60	9
XVII	32	92	52	-28	16	8	-44	-48	-32	0	-16	-16	-20	-32	24	-30	96	52	-36	8
XVIII	-36	-24	8	4	0	-2	52	78	-12	-4	36	-8	28	-24	-16	-14	42	-12	-40	9
XIX	-52	-52	-66	4	6	-6	-4	44	-66	-4	44	12	44	40	16	-46	44	-42	-32	4
	1	1	2	3	7	11	3	3	4	6	9	2	5	7	10	4	4	8	10	: 100

STRAT EGIE

MATRICE DES REGLEMENTS. DUEL, (VALEUR DU JEU = 0).

CHEF X (LIGNES)

VENTS
PERC. NORM.
H CORDES: PERC. CAISSE
.: CORDES: PIZZ., ETC...
CORDES: GLISS.
≡ CORDES: TENUES

(VENTS+PERC) SIN.

(VENTS+PERC + CORDES PERC) SIMULTANEMENT

I. Xénakis
ST/VENISE. 101062

ATREES for 10 players (1958–62)

Instrumentation: Flute, Clarinet, Bass Clarinet, Horn, Trumpet, Tenor Trombone, Percussion (Maracas, Suspended Cymbals, Gong, 5 Temple-blocks 4 Tom-toms, Vibraphone) 1 Violin, 1 Violoncello.

Duration: 15 minutes.

First performance: 1962. Paris. Conductor, K. Simonovic.

Publisher: Editions Française de Musique, O.R.T.F., Paris.

Explanation of the title: The inflexible laws of Necessity. Composed and performed in homage to Blaise Pascal, who with Fermat was one of the founders of the calculus of probabilities. This work makes use of the same stochastic programme as ST/10—1 and is calculated by the IBM 7090 Computer at the Place Vendôme. However, some licence was introduced in this case. (Cf. Gravesaner Blätter No. 26, Gravesano, Ticino, Switzerland, and Musiques Formelles, ed. Richard-Masse, Paris).

POLLA TA DHINA for children's chorus and small orchestra (1962)

Instrumentation: 20 children's voices, Piccolo, Flute, 2 Oboes, Clarinet, Bass Clarinet, Bassoon, Contrabassoon, 2 Horns, 2 Trumpets, 2 Tenor Trombones, Percussion and Strings (8,8,6,6,4).

Duration: 6 minutes.

Dedicated to Hermann Scherchen.

First performance: 1962. Stuttgart Festival of Light Music, which commissioned the work. Conductor, Hermann Scherchen.

Publisher: Edition Modern (Wewerka), Franz-Josephstrasse 2, 8 Munich 13, Germany.

Explanation of the title: The voices chant on one note the Greek text "Hymn to Mankind", taken from the Antigone of Sophocles. *Polla ta dhina* ("Many are the wonders") are the opening words of the text.

EONTA for Piano and 5 Brass instruments

Instrumentation: Piano solo, 2 Trumpets, 3 Tenor Trombones.

Duration: 18 minutes.

First performance: December 1964. Domaine Musicale, Paris.
Conductor, Pierre Boulez; Pianist, Yuji Takahashi.

Publisher: Boosey & Hawkes.

Explanation of the title: Eonta=Beings (Ionian dialect, neuter plural of the present participle of the verb to be). The work makes use of stochastic (probabilist) and symbolic (logistic) music. Certain parts, notably the early part of the piano solo, were calculated by the IBM 7090 computer at the Place Vendôme, Paris. This piece was composed in Berlin in 1963–4. The title is in Cypriot syllabic characters of Creto-mycenean origin which were lost for 24 centuries and only recently deciphered.

HIKETIDES (The Suppliants) for choir of 50 women, who also play percussion instruments, and 10 orchestral instruments

Instrumentation: 50 altos or mezzo-sopranos (with percussion), 2 Trumpets, 2 Trombones, 2 Violins, 2 Violoncellos, 2 Doublebasses.

Duration: 15 or 30 minutes (without choir or with choir).

First performance: 1964. At the Theatre at Epidaurus, Athens Festival.

Publisher: Boosey & Hawkes.

This is music for Aeschylus' tragedy of the same name. The 50 women of the chorus are armed with special percussion instruments: castanets, triangles of every different size, maracas, bells, jingles, side-drums. They dance, sing or declaim, accompanying themselves with these instruments so that the sounds move around from place to place (this idea is used again and expanded in TERRETEKTORH, 1965–66).

AKRATA for 16 wind instruments (1964–65)

Instrumentation: Piccolo, Oboe, Clarinet in B♭, Clarinet in E♭, Bass Clarinet, Bassoon, 2 Contra-bassoons, 2 Horns, 3 Trumpets, 2 Tenor Trombones, Tuba.

Duration: 11 minutes.

Dedicated to Olga and Serge Koussevitsky and commissioned by the Library of Congress, Washington.

First performance: June 1966. At the English Bach Festival, Oxford. Conductor, Charles Bruck.

Publisher: Boosey & Hawkes.

Explanation of the title: "Pure" (neuter plural). This work is of an extra-temporal architecture, based on the theory of groups of transformations. Use is made in it of the theory of Sieves, a theory which annexes the congruences modulo Z and which is the result of an axiomatic theory of the universal structure of music. In it, use is made of complex numbers (imaginary ones). Cf. La Nef No. 29, Paris, 1967.

TERRETEKTORH for large orchestra of 88 players scattered among the audience (1965–66)

Instrumentation: 2 Flutes, Piccolo, 3 Oboes, Clarinet in B♭, Clarinet in E♭, Bass Clarinet, 2 Bassoons, Contrabassoon, 4 Horns, 4 Trumpets, 4 Tenor Trombones, Tuba, Percussion (3 Players) and Strings (16,14,12,10,8).

In addition each of the 88 players must have: 1 Wood-block, 1 Whip, 1 Maracas, 1 "Acme" siren-whistle. To avoid having to gather together each time so large a number of instruments, the complete percussion material exists at O.R.T.F. Paris, eventually for hire.

Duration: 15 minutes.

Dedicated to Hermann Scherchen and Pierre Souvtchinsky.

First performance: 3rd April, 1966. Royan Festival of Contemporary Music, France. Philharmonic Orchestra of O.R.T.F., under the direction of Hermann Scherchen.

Explanation of the title: TEKT=construction (construction by action)—ORH=action of—TERRE: a prefix amplifying the roots of the word that follows. This work proposes two fundamental innovations which should entirely alter the conception of writing for, and listening to, the orchestra.

(a) The quasi-stochastic sprinkling of the orchestral musicians among the audience. The orchestra is in the audience and the audience is in the orchestra. Preferably the public should sit on camp-stools given out at the entrace to the hall. Each musician of the orchestra should be seated on an individual, but unresonant, daïs with his desk and instruments. The hall where the piece is to be performed should be cleared of every movable object that might cause aural or visual obstruction (seats, stage, etc.) A large ball-room having (if it were circular) a minimum diameter of 45 yards would serve in default of a new kind of architecture which will have to be devised for all types of present-day music, for neither amphitheatres, and still less normal theatres or concert-halls, are suitable.

The scattering of the musicians brings in a radically new kinetic conception of music which no modern electro-acoustical means could match. For if it is not possible to imagine 90 magnetic tape tracks relaying to 90 loud speakers disseminated all over the auditorium, on the contrary it is quite possible to achieve this with a classical orchestra of 90 musicians. The musical composition will thereby be entirely enriched throughout the hall both in spatial dimension and in movement. The speeds and accelerations of the movement of the sounds will be realized, and new and powerful functions will be able to be made use of, such as logarithmic or Archimedean spirals, in time and geometrically. Ordered or disordered sonorous masses, rolling one against the other like waves . . . etc., will be possible.

TERRETEKTORH is thus a "Sonotron": an accelerator of sonorous particles, a disintegrator of sonorous masses, a synthetiser. It puts the sound and the music all around the listener and close up to him. It tears down the psychological and auditive curtain that separates him from the players when positioned far off on a pedestal, itself frequently enough placed inside a box. The orchestral musician rediscovers his responsibility as an artist, as an individual.

(b) The orchestral colour is moved towards the spectrum of dry sounds, full of noise, in order to broaden the sound-palette of the orchestra and to give maximum effect to the scattering, mentioned above. For this effect, each of the 90 musicians has, besides his normal string or wind instrument, three percussion instruments, viz. Wood-block, Maracas, and Whip as well as small Siren-whistles, which are of three registers and give sounds resembling flames. So if necessary,

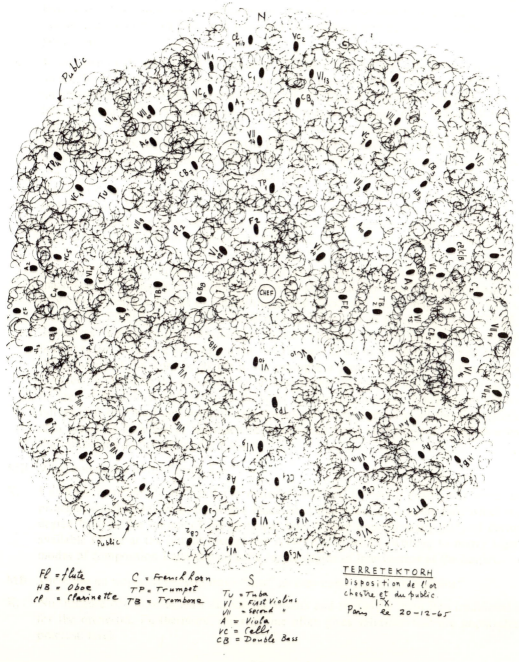

Fl = flute
HB = Oboe
Cl = Clarinette

C = French horn
TP = Trumpet
TB = Trombone

Tu = Tuba
VI = First Violins
VII = second "
A = Viola
VC = Celli
CB = Double Bass

TERRETEKTORH
Disposition de l'orchestre et du public.
I.X.
Paris le 20-12-65

a shower of hail or even a murmuring of pine-forests can encompass each listener, or in fact any other atmosphere or linear concept either static or in motion. Finally the listener, each one individually, will find himself either perched on top of a mountain in the middle of a storm which attacks him from all sides, or in a frail barque tossing on the open sea, or again in a universe dotted about with little stars of sound, moving in compact nebulae or isolated.

ORESTEIA (Music for The Oresteia of Aeschylus) (1965–66) for Mixed Chorus and Chamber Orchestra

Instrumentation: Piccolo, Oboe, Clarinet, Bass Clarinet, Contrabassoon, Horn, Trumpet, Piccolo Trumpet in B♭, Tenor Trombone, Tuba, Percussion (of all kinds, classical and unusual), Violoncello.

Duration: 100 minutes.

First performance: June 1966. At the Ypsilanti (Michigan, U.S.A.). Festival, by whom the work was commissioned for their Greek Theatre.

ORESTEIA SUITE (Concert version of above) for Mixed Chorus and Chamber Orchestra

Instrumentation: Piccolo, Oboe, Clarinet, Bass Clarinet, Contrabassoon, Horn, Trumpet, Piccolo Trumpet in B♭, Tenor Trombone, Tuba, Percussion (of all kinds, classical and unusual), Violoncello.

Duration: 50 minutes.

Publisher: Boosey & Hawkes.

POLYTOPE

Instrumentation: 4 identical orchestras, each consisting of:—
Piccolo, Clarinet in E♭, Contrabass Clarinet, Contrabassoon, Trumpet in C, Tenor Trombone, Percussion (1 player): Large Gong, Japanese Wood-block, 4 Tom-toms, 4 Violins, 4 Violoncellos.

Duration: 6 minutes.

First performance: 1967, Montreal.

Publisher: Boosey & Hawkes.

Explanation: The four orchestras are placed at the four cardinal points in the concert area. The music was created to accompany the Luminous Poem which Xenakis conceived for the French pavilion at Expo '67, Montreal. But it may be performed on its own. The convex sounds form a musical material of great contrasts, as in Terretektorh.

CHAMBER MUSIC

ST/4 for String Quartet (1965–62)

Duration: 12 minutes.

First performance: 1962. Paris The Bernede String Quartet.

Explanation of the title: As shown by its components: ST/4—1,080262. ST=stochastic music. 4—1=first work for 4 instruments. 080262=8th February 1962, the date when this work was calculated by the electronic brain.

ST/4 is a version for four strings of the work ST/10 for 10 instruments, which was calculated by the electronic brain 7090 IBM in Paris in obedience to a special stochastic (probabilist) "programme" devised by Xenakis. This "programme" was derived from the thesis of "Minimum of Rules of Composition", which had already been formulated in ACHORRIPSIS, but it was not until four years later that it became possible to have it "mechanised" at IBM-France.

The "programme" is a complex of stochastic laws which the composer had been introducing into musical composition for a number of years. He ordered the electronic brain to define all the sounds of a sequence, previously calculated, one after the other. First, the time of its occurrence, next its class of timbre (arco, pizzicato, glissando, etc.), its instrument, its pitch, the gradient of its glissando where that occurs, the duration and dynamic of the emission of sound. This Quartet makes use of every way of playing these stringed instruments, notably those introduced by Xenakis in his orchestral works METASTASEIS and PITHOPRAKTA, such as tapping the backs of the instruments, glissandi, pizzicato and *col legno* taps on the strings.

For further information, see "A la recherche d'une Musique stochastique", Xenakis' article in the revue Gravesaner Blätter No.'s 11/12 of 1958; also chapter I of the book "Musiques Formelles", also by Xenakis, ed. Richard-Masse, Paris.

For the programme in Fortran language, see Gravesaner Blätter No. 26, Gravesano, Ticino, Switzerland.

MORSIMA-AMORSIMA for 4 instruments (1956–62) for Piano, Violin, Violoncello, Doublebass

Duration: 11 minutes.

First performance: 1962. Athens, under the direction of Lukas Foss.

Explanation of the title: Moros=Fate, death. Morsima=that which comes from Fate. Amorsima (*a* being the negative particle) that which does not come from Fate. It is the result of the same programme as for ST/10 (see above) but for a different combination of instruments.

HERMA for Piano Solo (1960–61)

Duration: 9 minutes.

Dedicated to Yuji Takahashi.

First performance: 1962. Tokyo. Yuji Takahashi.

Explanation of the title: "Bond", "foundation", "embryo". This piece is based on logical operations imposed upon classes of pitches; this is why I call this music "symbolic". Starting from the four classes defined in the score, others can be formed *outside of time,* as a result of the complementary relationship (negation), e.g., class A; the negation of A is written in the score $\bar{A}$; also as a result of the operation of union (disjunction) and of intersection (conjunction). Union is shown symbolically by the sign+, and intersection by the juxtaposition of letters. Union corresponds to *or* and intersection to *and.* Thus A+B signifies that class in which the elements belong either to A or B; AB indicates the class in which the elements belong to classes A and B at the same time. The classes in this piece are defined solely within the realm of pitch.

NOMOS ALPHA for Violoncello Solo (1965–66)

Duration: 17 minutes.

Dedication: "A la mémoire d'Aristoxène de Tarente, de Evariste Galois et de Felix Klein". Specially written for S. Palm.

First performance: May 1966. Bremen. Soloist, S. Palm.

Explanation of the title: "Rules, laws", but also in music "a special particular melody" and sometimes "mode". Symbolic music for solo 'cello, posssesing an extra-temporal architecture based on the theory of groups of transformations. In it use is made of the theory of "sieves", a theory which annexes the congruences modulo Z and which is the result of an axiomatic theory of the universal structure of music. This work is an act of homage to the imperishable work of Aristoxenes of Taranto, musician, philosopher and mathematician and founder of the Theory of Music, of Evariste Galois, mathematician and founder of the Theory of Groups and of Felix Klein, his worthy successor. Written for Siegfried Palm, it was commissioned by Hans Otte of Bremen Radio.

AMORSIMA—MORSIMA for 10 players (1956–62)
ATREES for 10 players (1958–62)   *for details see*
EONTA for Piano and 5 Brass instruments (1963–64)   WORKS FOR ORCHESTRA

ELECTRO-MAGNETIC WORKS

DIAMORPHOSES Electro-magnetic music. 1957. O.R.T.F. Paris. 7 minutes.

CONCRET PH (1958) Electro-magnetic music for the Philips pavilion at Brussels Exposition 1958, O.R.T.F. Paris. 2½ minutes.

ANALOGIQUES A and B (1959) Music for 9 strings and for magnetic tape. Editions Françaises de Musique, O.R.T.F., Paris.

ORIENT OCCIDENT (1960) Music for the UNESCO film of the same title. 12 minutes.

BOHOR Electro-magnetic (1962) O.R.T.F. Paris. For 8 tracks. 24 minutes.

RECORDINGS

METASTASEIS
PITHOPRAKTA   Orchestre National de l'O.R.T.F., conducted by Maurice Le Roux.

EONTA   Yuji Takahashi (solo piano) and the Ensemble Instrumental de Musique Contemporaine de Paris, conducted by Konstantin Simonovic.

Chant du Monde—Mono LDX 8368—Stereo LDXA 48368

This recording was awarded the GRAND PRIX NATIONAL DU DISQUE 1966 by the Académie du Disque Français.

"A spectacular recording" (Arts).

"A disc which does justice to one of the most personal and most convincing composers of our time" (Le Nouvel Observateur).

"No product of a limited system, nor of the laboratory, but undeniable poetry. This record brings understanding of Xenakis" (L'Humanite).

"The music of Xenakis adds up to a musical phenomenon" (Le Journal Musical Français).

ST/4 for String Quartet

    The Bernede String Quartet, Paris.

    Experimental disc, Studio Hermann Scherchen, Gravesano (1965), published together with No. 26 of the Gravesaner Blätter.

DIAMORPHOSES (Electro-magnetic Music)

    7-inch disc. Boite à Musique, Paris.

ANALOGIQUE A & B⎫ Philips "Panorama of Concrete Music". Mono A 00567L—Stereo 835487
CONCRET PH   ⎭ AY.

ORIENT-OCCIDENT (Electro-magnetic music)

    Philips "Experimental Music". Mono A 00565L—Stereo 835485 AY.

ST/4, ATREES, MORSIMA—AMORSIMA, NOMOS ALPHA

    recordings in preparation (Pathé-Marconi).

BIBLIOGRAPHY OF THE WRITINGS OF XENAKIS

BOOKS

  "Musiques Formelles"—in French. (Editions Richard-Masse 1963—7 Place St. Sulpice, Paris VIᵉ)

MAGAZINE ARTICLES

 (1) **Music**

  "GRAVESANER BLÄTTER", Gravesano, Ticino, Switzerland

    no. 1, La Crise de la musique sérielle

    no. 6, Calcul des probabilités et Musique

    nos. 11 et 12, A la recherche d'une Musique Stochastique

    no. 18, Eléments de Musique Stochastique

    no. 19, Eléments de Musique Stochastique

    no. 20, Eléments de Musique Stochastique

    no. 21, Eléments de Musique Stochastique

    no. 22, Eléments de Musique Stochastique

    no. 23, Musique Stochastique

    no. 26, Programme en Fortran de Musique Stochastique (issued together with the disc of ST/4)

    no. 29, Vers une philosophie de la Musique

    In French, English and German.

  "NUTIDA MUSIK", (Swedish Radio publication)

    no. 4, 1958/59, Les Trois Paraboles

    no. 6, 1958, Sur un Geste électronique

  "LA REVUE MUSICALE" (Richard-Masse, 7 Place St. Sulpice, Paris VIᵉ)

    no. 244, 1959, Expériences Musicales "Sur un geste électronique". In French.

  "REVUE D'ESTHETIQUE" (J. Vrin, 6 Place de la Sorbonne, Paris Vᵉ)

    Tome 14, Fasc. III et IV, Juillet-Décembre 1961, "Musique Stochastique". In French.

"MARCATRE" (Via Lazio 9, Rome)

no. 3, February 1964, "Musique Stochastique" (translation of the "Revue d'Esthétique" into Italian).

"MUSIC EAST AND WEST" (Tokyo)

Conference Reports on 1961 Tokyo East-West Music Encounter. Stochastic Music. In English.

"PREUVES" (18 avenue de l'Opéra Paris 1er)

November 1965 "La voie de la recherche et de la question". In French.

"MODULOR 2" by Le Corbusier (Ed. Architecture d'Aujourd'hui) 1955.

Interview in "ONGAKU GEIJUTSU" (Tokyo)
no. 6, 1961. In Japanese

"SLOVENSKA HUDBA" (Bratislava)

1964. Article in Czech.

"RUGH MUZYCZNY" (Warsaw)

1961–62. Writings on Debussy and Xenakis. In Polish.

"LE POEME ELECTRONIQUE LE CORBUSIER" (Editions de Minuit, Paris). 1958.

"LA NEF", no. 29, January 1967. "Vers une métamusique". In French.

(2) Architecture

COUVENT DE LA TOURETTE contained in Le Corbusier's book "Modulor 2" (Ed. Architecture d'Aujourd'hui). 1955.

L'ARCHITECTURE DU PAVILION PHILIPS in "Revue Technique Philips", vol. 20 1958–59.

LE PAVILION PHILIPS in "Gravesaner Blätter no. 9".

"LE MODULOR DE LE CORBUSIER" in "Gravesaner Blätter no. 10".

"A PROPOS DE LE CORBUSIER" in "Gravesaner Blätter no. 27/28".

"A PROPOS DE LE CORBUSIER" "Aujourd'hui, Art et Architecture", November 1965.

"LA VILLE COSMIQUE ("COSMIC CITY"). A study of polytopic urbanism in "L'Urbanism, Utopies et Réalitiés" by Françoise Choay. In French. (Editions de Seuil, Paris, 1965). In an English translation by J. Ashberg in "Art and Literature" no. 10 (SELA, 1000 Lausanne, Switzerland).

COURSES AND CONFERENCES GIVEN BY XENAKIS

Sweden, France, Germany, England, Holland, Poland, U.S.A., Canada, Argentina, Brazil, Philippines, Japan.